Correct
MANNERS
&
ETIQUETTE

Developing a pleasing personality/behaviour

Seema Gupta

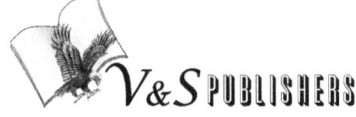

Published by:

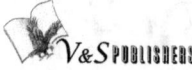
V&S PUBLISHERS

F-2/16, Ansari road, Daryaganj, New Delhi-110002
☎ 23240026, 23240027 • *Fax:* 011-23240028
Email: info@vspublishers.com • *Website:* www.vspublishers.com

Branch: Hyderabad
5-1-707/1, Brij Bhawan (Beside Central Bank of India Lane)
Bank Street, Koti, Hyderabad - 500 095
☎ 040-24737290
E-mail: vspublishershyd@gmail.com

Follow us on:

All books available at **www.vspublishers.com**

© **Copyright:** V&S PUBLISHERS
ISBN 978-93-813841-5-2
Edition: 2012

Printed at: Param Offseters, Okhla, New Delhi-110020

PUBLISHER'S NOTE

In line with a number of books on *Personality Development,* V & S Publishers have come out with the revised edition of the book, **Correct Manners & Etiquette** written by the well-known author, psychotherapist and counsellor, Seema Gupta. The book is a complete guide on the Right Manners and Etiquette that a person should practise to develop a good behaviour and a pleasing personality. What should be his dress code and posture, his language, his way of greeting people, his conduct while working with his colleagues in office or at home, telephone manners, written communication, etc., all these and many more have been elaborately discussed and explained by the author.

It is a fact that children should be taught good manners and etiquette, right from their childhood to grow up into a person with a pleasing behaviour and personality. It is the responsibility of the parents, elders and teachers to guide them and set examples for them by their own conduct and actions.

This book is meant for readers of all ages, particularly for youngsters and children, for a well-mannered person is always welcome and liked by everyone in a society. By reading this book, one can learn the acumen of polished behaviour and groom oneself accordingly to outshine in all spheres of life. Good mannerisms and etiquette can impress people instantly and you can be a winner in whichever circumstance or field you are in. Hence, this book is a must for all those who aim to make it big in their lives and win everyone's heart!

PREFACE

The other day I went to a restaurant with my friends for lunch. Though the place was full, we managed to get a table. The waiters were rushed off their feet, scurrying from table to table. Over the noise in the restaurant, we heard a 'Shish...shish'ing sound coming from a corner. On turning towards it, we found it was a group of business executives trying to attract the waiter's attention. One of them, apparently getting restless with the delay in service, was summoning the waiter by clicking his fingers and making strange sounds to attract his attention. When the waiter finally reached this table, the disgust on his face was quite evident.

What a glaring contrast there was between this group and a couple sitting near our table, who, too, were trying to get the waiter's attention. It was the manner in which they went about it that was so different. Waiting patiently till he caught the waiter's eye, this man held up his index finger up and said "Excuse me". The waiter promptly came to their table and took their order with all due courtesy and smiles. The marked difference in both behaviours probably never occurred to the impatient group. So used to getting their own way at once, it may never have crossed their minds that there could be something wrong in the manner they went about it.

Such incidents are commonplace and so are ill-mannered people. Actually, most people whose behaviour strikes others as bad or ill manners have conducted themselves in this manner for so long that it has turned into a habit and comes naturally to them. It is only when they come across someone with better etiquette that comparison takes place and the realisation strikes a home run.

Good manners today are in a state of flux as they were never before. One can no longer turn to the rules that worked 50 or maybe even 20 years ago. Formal and rigid in outlook, they have little to do with the casual lifestyles that prevail today. However, there is one factor that has remained constant. And this is that your actions and behaviour will be observed by everyone; and unfortunately, a wrong first impression is more lasting than any number of good deeds that may follow. You will be observed equally by strangers as well as by people who matter to you. And, I am sure, that at least for the latter, you would like to be at your best.

Sound manners and good etiquette are based on the three most endearing of all human traits — kindness, thoughtfulness and consideration for others. That is why teaching your children basic manners takes top priority. It is your duty to show them the right path and they only learn what you teach them or emulate whatever you do yourself. At this young age, any adult with whom they are in close contact is their ideal and they try to imitate that person in every way — be it greeting someone cheerfully or hiding in your bedroom to avoid that person; digging your nose, cleaning your ears or scratching your head in public or in the privacy of your bathroom — children have an uncanny sense of perception and memory. So be a good model for them. Teach them the best of manners just like you provide them with the best of food, clothes and education.

This will help you achieve your goal. It helps you to conform and encourages you to do the right thing at the right time. Etiquette and manners at home, with visitors, guests, at the office, introductions and greetings, various forms of address, written communications, salutations, conduct during various ceremonies like births, weddings, anniversaries, deaths and funerals, parties, picnics are all dealt with in this book in detail.

Within any social ambience, if you find yourself in an unfamiliar situation, this book will help you come out of it. Just go through it and be assured of smooth sailing henceforth.

— *Seema Gupta*

CONTENTS

ETIQUETTE — THE KEYWORD

Lord Tredegar knew exactly how to handle a habit of several years. One of his servants reported this incident — "I remember the morning when Lord Tredegar was taken exceedingly ill. Instead of the usual nod of his head to me on my arrival, he said, 'Cronin, I think I'm dying'."

The years-old habit could not be amended in a moment. I knew that even Lord Tredegar in his more collected moments would not wish it so. So correctly I replied, 'Very good, my Lord', Thereafter, the normal silence between us was reestablished to our mutual satisfaction.

*E*tiquette and good manners are acquired through constant practice. They are inculcated from childhood and become habits by the time we grow up. Remember the times when you were irritated by your mother's constant nagging to clean up the mess in your room. But she was only trying to help you by merely cultivating the good habit of tidiness in you — such is the case with good manners.

Can the ability to get along with others be learnt or is it a trait that you are born with? While there are people who appear to be born charmers, most of us have to learn how to relate to others. Even the charmers often find that they have to refine their skills of communication. Do we all not envy that charming, selfconfident fellow who moves with grace? He has the ability to turn even the most embarrassing situations into playful witty moments by his intellect and good-natured humour. A person with a fine sense of etiquette exudes confidence. He is able to put everybody at ease, unmindful of their social rank or status.

Several years ago, John D. Rockfeller said, "The ability to get along with people is as purchaseable a commodity as sugar and coffee, and I pay more for that ability than any under the sun."

Good manners are essential in building good relationships with other people and they can ensure that you have a steady supply of support and cooperation.

The practice of etiquette can be traced back to the times of kings and emperors where the courtiers bowed before the royal family. The elders received due respect and youngsters never spoke harshly to their parents.

Over the centuries, considerable emphasis has been placed in various societies on the proper forms of behaviour. Across the globe, career diplomats, armed force personnels, business executives, and even politicians are put through stiff training where even the minutest of details in etiquette is not excused. Even in our social circle, have we not noticed that it is the persons with pleasing mannerisms who are the most popular? No doubt, they have an edge over others. Although in the informality that prevails today, interest in codified behaviour has declined, yet at our parties, wedding cremonies, funerals, deaths, seminars or business meetings, we do observe certain basic acceptable norms of human behaviour.

By cultivating correct mannerisms and using them constantly, we are sure to be able to tackle various social occasions with confidence. Our skills in the areas of courtesy, politeness and etiquette can never go wasted.

A senior British diplomat was on his way to a Diplomtic meeting in London when his young secretary began complaining about etiquette and diplomatic Bologna.

"Isn't it a lot of hot air?", asked the secretary. "All etiquette is hot air, my dear", answered the wise diplomat. "But that's what's in our automobile tyres and see how it eases the bumps."

POSTURE

It is bearing, disposition, demeanour and poise that determine the pattern of our lives. A man may stand erect or stoop, he may sit smartly or lazily, he may speak nicely and soothingly or crudely — these and their variations are all part of good manners. A good posture indicates your good upbringing and the poised human body is one that ought to look as nature meant it to do so — upright, straight and beautiful. It is in the poised and healthy body that the poised and healthy mind is most often found.

Sitting Pretty

Anyone and everyone always sits down but graceful sitting begins with the manner in which you approach your chair. The first thing to bear in mind is that the act of sitting down should be done quietly. You should not plonk yourself down on a chair or scramble for a seat. Deliberate controlled movements are needed.

Hands: While sitting down, hands are particularly important. It is your hands that pose a problem, if you do not know what to do with them. Your nervousness may be apparent from the tremor through your hands. You should therefore learn how to place your hands properly either on the hands of the chair, or on your lap, or else they will get in your way and look very ungainly. Hands that are relaxed give you an aura of serenity and poise. Avoid jerky movements.

Legs: Legs also play an important role in your self-composure, poise and confidence. Do not shake or jerk your legs constantly. Besides being an unwelcome distraction to others, they look indecent. The cardinal rule for a lady when she sits is to keep her knees together.

Talking while sitting: When carrying on a conversation while sitting, you should be careful that your body movements are well synchronized so that they project a good personality. These movements become an aid to your posture. Smiles, acknowledgements, nods and so on should be combined with all these.

Standing

Standing is sometimes more difficult than sitting. One reason is that it causes more strain. There are various modes of standing—

(a) Standing straight with your hands hanging loosely at the sides.

(b) With your feet a little apart and your hands clasped behind you — this is termed standing at ease.

(c) Slight stooping or bowing as a mark of respect.

(d) Some people prefer standing with their hands on their hips. This is the worst form of standing and indicates that the person has no manners at all. It not only shows disrespect to others but also portrays an indifferent aggressive attitude.

(e) If you are dealing with a V.I.P., it would be better to adopt a posture of alertness instead of one of laid-back serenity.

Talking while standing: When you are holding a conversation with another person and both are standing, your attention should not be diverted. But if you are sitting when another person strikes up a conversation, you should get up immediately and talk to him. You should not let your attention be diverted elsewhere. The only

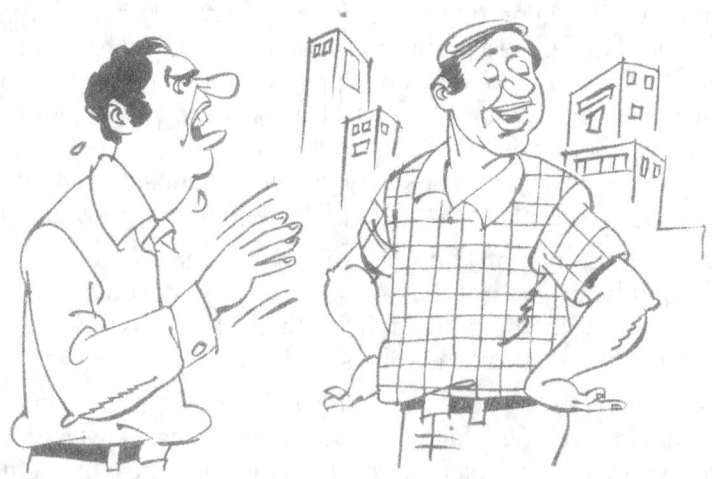

exception to the rule is if you are the host and have the responsibility of welcoming and seeing to the convenience of your guests, it is permissible for you to allow your attention to wander while in conversation.

Good Posture Habits

By teaching your child good posture habits, you have not only saved his physique but a lot of future embarrassment as well.

Sitting with a straight back, standing with ease and walking with the head held high are the basics of a good posture.

Posture is very closely associated with one's nature. If you sit erect, use your hands properly and know how to manage your legs while sitting in a group, you portray an image of a confident and composed person. Fumbling with your things unnecessarily, shaking your legs, touching your nose, ears or hair, playing with your fingers — these give you away by demonstrating your nervousness. Correct your child whenever you find him stooping. Stop him firmly if he is getting into the habit of shaking his legs while in conversation. Teach him how to walk and sit gracefully. You can make him understand the importance of a good posture by showing him as two different persons with good and bad posture habits respectively. The difference is so obvious that it will not be difficult to explain the importance of good posture to him.

Impatience : Enemy of Good Posture

Have you ever noticed that person pacing up and down the floor, scratching his ear, poking his nose, cracking his fingers, or looking at his watch every 10 seconds? What did you say? "He is in a big hurry." For what? No Sir, he is only waiting for a table in this restaurant, for which the manager has already told him that it would take 10 minutes. He is just a very impatient man. And this is revealed in his posture habits. He forgets all the basics of good posture as this devil of a habit — impatience — takes over. So be warned, even if you are an impatient kind of person, hide it tactfully and maintain your poise and charm. Remember, a delay of a few minutes will not cause havoc in your life. The sky will still be there when you look up five minutes later.

Do's and Don'ts

Keep your back and head straight and don't stoop. Talk without shifting around in your chair. Sit with knees close together — never wide apart. Don't take up more space than required. Avoid making unnecessary and flamboyant gestures.

Don't sit too close to the persons on either side of you. If walking in a crowd, try keeping pace with others — don't lag behind or stride ahead. Don't stop suddenly — others will walk into you.

If walking with a lady, walk on the outer side somewhat protectively. Don't walk too fast so that she has to run to keep pace with you.

DRESS-CODE

(This chapter may be skipped by men as it focusses on the fairer sex.)

Dress to suit your figure, face and personality. Clothing — no matter how artfully designed, how perfectly made, how fashionably styled — must always be judged on the basis of its relationship to the wearer. When selecting clothes and accessories, you must have a complete understanding of yourself, your figure, face and personality — this will help you achieve distinction and personal attractiveness.

> *Costly the raiment as thy purse can afford,*
> *Rich but not gaudy...*
> *For apparel oft proclaims the man."*
>
> — *Shakespeare*

*G*ood taste may be defined as a refined look, leaning more towards the conservative and simple than a flamboyant spectacular look. Remember these points.

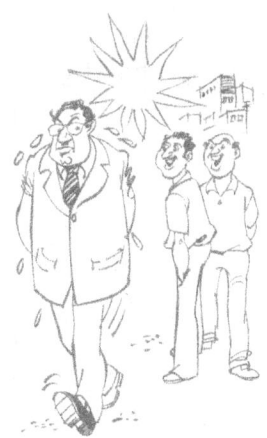

15

Avoid offensively revealing clothes. Never be ostentatious or over-ornamented. Avoid fancy jewelry for day-time wear. Do not follow fashion blindly. Make sure you are neat and clean.

Simplicity and Good Taste

Status symbols have never had more power than they have today. Titan watches, Action shoes, Big Joe's T-shirts, Kala Mandir sarees, City Look sweaters and Weekender shirts are taking over. But do not panic, if you cannot afford them. It is still possible to look good without investing so much in either your apparel or accessories. It is preferable to carry a good though small leather purse than to carry an ostentatious, flashy and more expensive one from Cottage Emporium.

A well-stitched reasonably priced *salwar* suit is much more appealing than a tightly fitting gaudy outfit from an expensive shop.

Natural fibres such as cotton, wool and silk are not only stylish but are also classic fibres that are acceptable in any place.

Select a good quality material and have it stitched by reliable tailor.

Flatter your figure and skin: A critical self-analysis is essential for you to get fully acquainted with your own body structure.

Slim figures: A slim, perfectly proportioned figure will have no problem with clothes. It is the overweight or too-thin that must be careful.

Plump figures: Those overweight should avoid horizontal lines, pleats, ribbing and tucking, contrasting colours, accentuating belts, yokes, etc. Instead they should go in for vertical lines, stripes, button front-closing from neck to hem.

Thin figures: The too-thin girl must wear garments that add to her figure giving an illusion of fullness.

Colours

As far as colours go, let us put them into the divisions give above.

Plump girls: Overweight girls/women should go in for staple colours of black, navy brown, or dark grey. Deep reds, darktoned greens, low-keyed purples also suit her. She should avoid shocking pink, fire-engine red, brilliant whites. The overweight should definitely avoid spotted prints, shiny finish and go in for small, patterned prints in muted colour combinations.

Thin girls: A thin girl on the other hand can wear staple colours but in heavier textures and contrasting lines that will seem to fill her out. A petite girl should never wear large or widely spaced prints.

Fitting In

Well-tailored clothes with appropriate curves and seams is the key to a good fit — not so tight that they wrinkle everywhere and not so loose that they hang. A *salwar* suit or a midi looks best when properly fitted. Most women have this misconception that they need only two or three blouses in basic colours to go with all their sarees. They also do not give much importance to the fitting of the blouse. An unmatched badly fitted blouse or an ankle-length pet-ticoat mars the beauty of even the most expensive saree.

Colour Blending

Colour blending is a very important boost to one's personality. If you are fair, all colours will suit you, especially pastel colours such as pale pink, blue, lemon, beige, cream, light green etc. For a wheatish and dark complexion, slightly dark colours are used.

Colour combination is an important aspect of dressing. Most women go wrong by using one blouse (usually black) with all the sarees. If you can spend a bundle on a saree, why not make it look more presentable by investing one-tenth of its cost in accessories? Men too should be careful about their colour combinations. Oranges, pinks, yellows, reds and greens are considered ladies' colours. Men should avoid them. Their best colours are grey, beige, blue and at-tributes of their different hues.

Although age groups used to matter earlier, these days all colours are worn by people despite their age group. A few years back, it was believed that dull grey shades, all light colours and various shades of cream belonged to the older generation, whereas all bright colours were meant for young people. However, with changing times, these rules have undergone a tremendous change. Today, if you buy a pink saree with a navy blue border for your mother, she will not give it to your wife, saying it's not her age to wear such colours. Instead, she will wear it quite happily.

However, there is no denying that sober colours do belong to the upper age group (say, above 40), as they indicate their maturity and bright and gaudy colours and dresses adapt well with young ones and children who are full of youth and bubbling with energy. Thus, their brightness and freshness matches best with the bright colours. Children, however, can wear any colour. But their best bet is bright colours, since childhood represents freedom from all worries and troubles, a carefree attitude, and so do these colours.

Accessories

Purses: A purse is a major accessory for women and should be bought keeping in mind your requirements. A leather purse always looks better than that of foam leather. There are different purses for different occasions and purposes. If, for example, you have a baby and you need to carry his water bottle and a few other things in your bag, a clutch purse will not serve the purpose. It is better in such a case to buy a large leather bag, spacious enough to hold all these things. Keep the small beaded clutch purse for social evenings. A smart medium-sized bag with a shoulder strap should be kept for going to office.

Do not overload your bag. It is never considered good manners if you spend half an hour searching for your hanky scattering your belongings all over the place. A bulging bag is very inelegant.

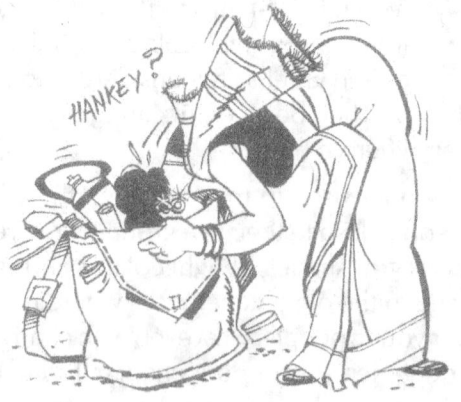

Shoes: Buy shoes to go with your outfit rather than buying them at random and impulsively and then trying to make them match your clothes. If you cannot afford many pairs, shoes in the three basic colours of black, brown, and maroon will do. Though high heels are very fashionable, do not go in for them unless you are confident and comfortable in stillettos. If your toes are pinched and feet cramped in tight-fitting shoes, the agony will be reflected on your face, besides making you irritable and snappy. If you are uncomfortable with the height of your heels, you will be unduly concerned about maintaining your balance and normal gait.

Handkerchiefs: A hanky should always be part of a person's wardrobe. Delicate lace-edged handkerchiefs for women and full-sized white ones with thin stripes for men should be used. They should be spotless, neatly ironed and changed daily. Remember even a little thing like a hanky goes a long way in building your personality and image.

Jewellery: Avoid the tendency to bedeck yourself with loads of jewellery in an effort to show off what you have. For college students, small studs in the ears or small rings, or a single bangle are sufficient. If you don't want to wear gold, the market is full of chunky, inexpensive jewellery ideal for the college student. Keep the gold for weddings and other special occasions.

Match your jewellery with your outfit, keeping the occasion in mind. You cannot wear junk stuff with a Kanjeevaram saree to a wedding. If you are going for a formal party or a reception, a gold set (earrings, chain, bangles, ring — all with the same design) may be worn. Precious stones embedded in gold look elegant when worn with a saree of the same hue. Diamonds and pearls go with everything.

Grooming: Needless to say that a well-dressed person falls short of the mark if he/she has not paid attention to personal grooming. Deodorants/anti-perspirants are a must in our hot climate. Do not drench yourself in perfume or after-shave. Spray on just enough so that a pleasant smell emanates from you.You need not go in for imported perfumes. A dash of rose water in your bath will do the trick.

The indigenous *ittars* are as good as any imported perfume.

The Appropriate Dress

We dress for various occasions — attending office, a wedding, dance, party, or just an informal get-together with old friends. Clothes reflect the aspirations and psyche of the wearer. Just as a heavily embroidered saree on a picnic would be totally inappropriate, so would minis or jeans be frowned upon if worn by a girl when she meeets her prospective in-laws or husband-to-be for the first time. The same bright red outfit which looked stunning at a party will be a total misfit at a funeral. A nicely starched *kurta-pyjama* will look out of place at a business meeting where every other person present is dressed in a suit. Likewise, the same clothes you prefer to wear to office will not do for a formal garden party.

For example, you have recently got married and your husband is happy to escort you around in clothes of your own choice, be it jeans, skirts, etc. But it would be insensitive of you to wear the same clothes when he takes you to meet his old, conservative grandfather for the first time. A saree or even a modest *salwar-kameez* would be most suited in this instance. In the same way, your husband should not insist on wearing his cut-off jeans or shorts when your relatives come visting.

This reminds me of an instance. A friend of mine, soon after completing her MA, got a job as a lecturer in a college. She did not give much consideration to what she wore on her first day at college and ended up wearing the first available garment she found — a skirt. The moment she entered the gates, she was accosted by a group of seniors who on mistaking her for a fresher began ragging her. Her protests fell on deaf ears and they thought she was fooling them by saying she was a lecturer. Later, when the truth came out, she was the laughing stock of the whole campus.

Dresses for Children

Compared to their elders, children have a wider variety of clothes to choose from. While boys can wear a pant-shirt or *kurta-pyjama* combination for non-formal occasions, and a coat-pant, *shervani* or safari for formal affairs, girls can have their pick from a range of lovely frocks to suit every occasion. They can also wear a *lehanga-chunri* to weddings. Girls have the advantage over boys as they can even wear pants or shorts. When choosing clothes for children, keep in mind their convenience and comfort. A silk *shervani* for your son in May or a thin cotton dress for your daughter in December will not do. Avoid dressing very small babies and infants in expensive silks and too many frills or flounces.

YOUR BEHAVIOUR

'You're better than anyone else.
Forget about learning to be polite.
You don't need to be polite.
You have a divine right.
The 'Thank you' and 'You are welcome' brigade
are there to serve.
If you must say something
A couple of grunts should suffice.'

*T*he day man left his abode in the jungle and proceeded to civilize himself and to lift himself to higher levels of achievement, was the point when social contacts began to have a special significance for him. Since then, he started judging himself and continues to strive for the betterment of his personality.

Your personality sets you apart from the rest of the crowd. It manifests itself in your taste, fine sense of aesthetics and your way of dealing with others. The basis for a good personality is a good behaviour pattern: how good you are at making friends, how you handle your rivals, your class and style, how you conduct yourself at public places and your inherent charm, decorum and dignity which can quietly affirm your good upbringing and background.

Making Right Friends
When life was simpler, friends had more in common and found it easier to be together. Relating to one's friends today is far more complex.

You are known by the company you keep. So be careful — if you are a submissive, quiet sort of chap but somehow managed to get friendly with the rowdy guys of the campus — you will be mistaken for one of them. Always remember, one good apple among the bad ones ends up getting spoilt itself.

Cutivating Charm

A charming person exudes friendship, warmth, bonhomie and fellowship around him. Charm is a way of evoking a positive response from others without having asked for it. It is this and other endearing qualities that cast their spell upon us when we come into contact with 'charming' individuals. We bask in their company and are drawn towards their magnetic personalities. What exactly is that undefinable quality that makes some people more endearing than others? Their poise, elegance, grace or a good sense of humour? These qualities may no doubt help but they are not essential prerequisites in a charming person. Then, is it physical charm? Need one be strikingly beautiful or dashingly handsome to be charming? Certainly not. In fact, many beautiful people are not at all charming. On the other hand, many plain, simple persons can be disarmingly charming.

Charming people appear to be naturally gifted. But charm can certainly be cultivated. And who wouldn't like to cultivate it? It doesn't take much to cultivate charm. A good knowledge of human behaviour and a fine sense of dealing with the situations around, is all that goes into it.

Imagine yourself to be a man and that as you were entering the elevator of a bank building, you saw a lady walking very fast towards it in an effort to get in before the door closed. You kept the button pressed till she entered the elevator. Inside, while she is trying to regain her composure, her bag falls down. You pick it up for her. She asks you to press the eighth floor button. Although you've already done so (since that is where you get off too), you nevertheless press it again. When the elevator stops at the eighth floor, you allow her to precede you. You both head for the same door. You hold the door open for her and enter only after she has gone in. Later, you meet her in the waiting lounge where only one chair is empty. You offer it to her.

From the look on her face, it is evident that she is thoroughly charmed by your behaviour. Long after you leave the bank, you will leave behind a good impression, causing her to spontaneously murmur: 'How charming!'.

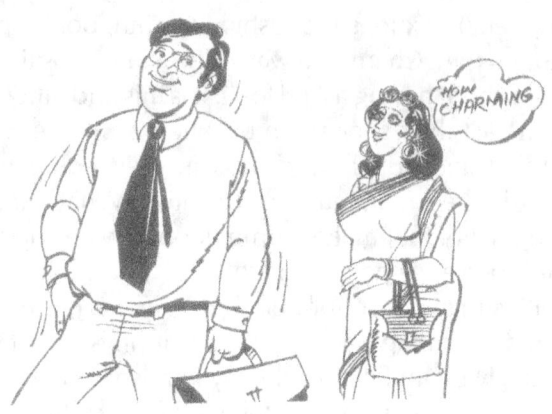

Class

What exactly is class? Here we are not talking of class as in any school or college. Class is a highly elusive quality like 'charm'. It is marked by a quiet stamp of authority, a binding presence and a bearing that announces your good breeding and refined taste. Who is said to have class? An executive in a chauffeur-driven Mercedes; intellectuals; celebrities? Class is much more than the public school syndrome with which it is usually confused. A good accent, diction, decent clothes, poise, intellect and fame do help, but do not constitute 'class' by themselves.

To determine whether you have class or not, you should ask yourself two questions. Are you able to carry yourself naturally without an iota of effort; and secondly, is it the people you meet who talk about your having class or vice versa? Always remember, those who are devoid of class continuously remind themselves and others of their possessing an abundance of it. There are individuals who talk of their most recent trip abroad to virtually anybody and everybody they meet. They will dwell on the restaurants and shopping arcades they visited, boast of their top connections, their imported household goods, etc., etc. Sounds familiar, doesn't it? This obviously is not class. Class is something which sets you a breed apart. Your modesty, honesty, good manners, politeness, sincerity towards relationships, genuine concern towards fellow human beings is more effective than any expensive material trappings to be eligible for that phrase 'a class apart'.

Road Sense

You couldn't eat your breakfast today. You were getting late for an early appointment. Look, there is a vendor near a red light selling *pao-bhaji*. But you can't stop suddenly like this in the middle of the road disrupting all the traffic around you. Indicate your intention to stop and then do so by the side of the road. Now you can buy your *pao-bhaji*. Stand aside and eat it and let the others like you take their turn. Do not eat while walking — remember, it's bad manners.

Your behaviour in the car or on the road is very important. If you are driving a vehicle, you are expected to know and above all follow traffic rules. Don't wait for the traffic police to *challan* you and show you the sign 'YOU'RE NOT A BULL. DON'T CHARGE WHEN YOU SEE RED.'

Honking, though not a crime, is as bad as having committed one. So don't honk unnecessarily. Also, don't try to attract a person's attention by the incessant blowing of your horn. Chances are, the whole neighbourhood, except for him, would be out. What about him? Well, he would be too ashamed to show his face to anyone, for having such an ill-mannered friend like you. Don't drive like a maniac on the road. You may give someone the fright of his life if, when speeding at 100 km/hr, you brake screechingly merely an inch away from him — only to ask for some directions. He would prefer to send you to the nearest police station.

Don't try to overtake another vehicle unless there is sufficient room to do so. First honk, get a clear signal, then go.

You must be thinking, what rubbish! These are only traffic rules. But it is not just that. These are all part of your behaviour pattern which, in time, becomes a part of your personality.

Enemies of Etiquette and Manners

We know very well what good manners are and the kind of good behaviour that is expected of us. But human nature is such that at times everything is shadowed by its one weakness — anger.

Anger: Anger in fact, is a common weakness which blinds you towards the good and bad, and the right and wrong. Even very civilized, well-behaved people can be found screaming and lashing out at others using the most obscene of language. How many times we have heard stories of famous film stars getting involved in a brawl just like that; or a politician finding himself in a police station, after having given in to his anger. So if you want to save your reputation, keep your temper in check. A very good antidose to it is — as soon as you feel your nerves are getting tense, take a deep breath and count to... well, 10, 20, ... 100. It depends on the intensity of your anger. Another good and easy (may not be so at that time) way out is — just turn around and make a graceful exit.

An apology after a showdown is a must to clear your heart but the best way is to prevent the showdown itself, while there is still time.

Do's and Don'ts

Respect your friends and friendship. Be natural in your dealing with others, don't be a show-off or pseudo.

Observe good manners even while on the road, like slowing down at zebra crossings, avoiding puddles so as not to splash passersbys, and not parking your vehicle just anywhere, blocking another's way.

HI ... HELLO!

"I'm Fzzzzz B zzzzz ... "
"Sorry, I couldn't get you!"
"I zzaid I'm Fzzzz Bzzzz ..."
"What's that?"
"Za'z my zame."
"What?"
"Fzzz Bzzz..."
"Mr Fzzz Bzzz ..."
"Zezz"
"Buzz off"

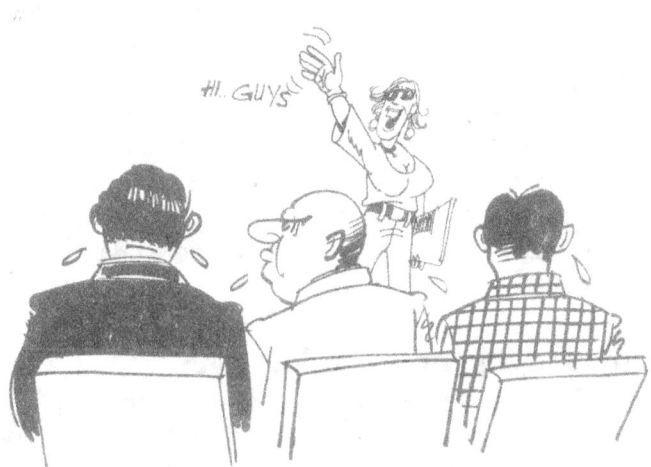

Introduction

Clarity should be the base of verbal introductions and referring to people. The general etiquette is straightforward: a man is introduced to a woman: the junior person between those of the same sex is introduced to the senior member. If a person introduces himself, he says as much, adding his first name and surname without a prefix. Sometimes, we tend to hope that the parties know one another and require no formal introduction. In a situation where the name of a person escapes the recollections of the introducer, one device is to turn to that person expectantly in an unspoken request to name themselves. On occasions when someone forgets your name, it is polite to jump in with a straightforward self-identification, making no reference to the lapse.

Business Introduction

Business introductions have become less rigid in recent years.

When introducing two peers to each other, say; "Seema Sharma, this is Anil Agarwal," or "Anil Agarwal, I would like you to meet Rohan Seth."

A man is generally presented to a woman; in business, this is definitely true if she holds a more prestigious position than he does. When a secretary, or administrative assistant, male or female, is introduced to a superior, however, he or she is presented to the superior. This means you say the superior's name first as follows: "Mr Agarwal, I would like to introduce Seema Sharma, my administrative assistant." In an informal office, the introduction might be: "Anil Agarwal, I would like you to meet Seema Sharma, my administrative assistant." If you are introducing a new employee to fellow workers, it is nice to add a statement about the new person, "Manoj Verma, I would like you to meet Rahul Pathak, who will be working with you in accounting."

Acknowledging an Introduction

There is really only one appropriate way to acknowledge an introduction and that is to say, very simply "How do you do." Try not to say, "Pleased to meet," "My pleasure," or "Pleased to make your acquaintance," all statements that may not be true ten minutes after you meet someone, especially in a business atmosphere.

In the Family

When introducing members of the family to new acquaintances, it is usual to mention any kinship ties. For example, "May I introduce my husband, Vivek?" "This is my wife, Anu." "I would like you to meet my son-in-law, Roshan.", or "Vinod, this is my daughter, Rina."

Instead of the customary 'ladies first', it is better to introduce men first. However, occasionally the roles are reversed as in: 'This is Anupam Bhattacharya and his gorgeous wife Kiran... she has all the money, right Kiran?"

A chuckle and you've made yourself clear and yet managed to keep to the rules by introducing the man first.

The etiquette of making introductions has become less rigid in recent years and could be due to the more casual styles prevailing among us.

You have gone to a party. You are sipping your Campa Cola when the host comes up to you with a girl of your age and says, "Rekha, I would like you to meet Renu Chaudhary." There is a mutual exchange of greetings and after a few minutes of polite talk, you both turn back to your respective groups. But what actually happened was that the names were lost in a splutter. You didn't catch it and in all probability, neither did she.

It often happens in social gatherings that in the course of numerous introductions, you end up not remembering who's who. But cheer up, there is nothing wrong with your memory. People to whom you have been introduced are also sailing in the same boat. On a second meeting, if you go 'Ummm...', she too is likely to stammer, 'I... well...'.

So instead of beating around the bush, the best way is to be straight-forward and simply say something like, "I am sorry but when we were being introduced, I didn't catch your name." Don't worry, she won't be offended and will quite willingly oblige you.

How to Introduce
To avoid such situations where neither of the parties catches each other's name, remember to pronounce names and surnames clearly to toss in a remark or two about them — like their profession, hobbies, etc. These are safe conversation openers.

Introducing Others
In a formal gathering: *You*: Mr Bhatia, meet Mr Gulati, a college friend of mine. He is with Modi Rubber as Finance Manager.

Mr Bhatia: How do you do.

In an informal gathering: You take a friend along to the group.

You: "This is Sudhir."

and then indicating each person go on... "This is Radhika, Ramesh, Ruchika..." and so on.

From those being introduced, a mere hello will suffice. After the formal introduction, somebody should draw the newcomer into the conversation by asking him a simple question like: 'What do you do?' or 'Have you been in Delhi for long?'

At a wedding: In a marriage function, the introductions should be done with context to the groom and the bride.

You: "Mrs Agarwal, this is Mrs Gupta, the bride's *mausi*. She also lives in Calcutta." Instead of "How do you do", the greeting here may be in the form of *'namaste'* or a mere nod of the head, indicating acknowledgement of the greeting.

Mrs Agarwal: "How nice. I also belong to Calcutta. Where do you stay in Calcutta?"

In college: You are walking along with a friend and happen to spot another friend unknown to the person you are with.

Excuse yourself by saying, "I won't be a minute"; or you could introduce them both to each other.

You: "Sudhir, meet Randhir, an old friend of mine. We were together in school."

Sudhir (friend): "Hello, how do you do."

Randhir (stranger):"Hello."

Introducing Yourself

Introducing oneself is much more difficult because here you are totally on your own and the other person is an absolute stranger to you.

At a formal party: It is better if the host introduces you but if he does not, then the best way is to use your business card. Hand it to the other person and say "Hello, I am Aneesh Gupta, Business Manager for Bharat Ltd."

Never ask for the other person's introduction without giving yours first. If you are an extrovent and enjoy making friends, go up to a person and introduce yourself by saying something like "Hello, I'm Ramesh Bhandari..." and set the ball rolling.

To a celebrity: You are invited to a party and to your good luck, you find your favourite actor, Amitabh Bachchan also there. If no one introduces you to him, you can directly go up to him and introduce yourself: "Hello, I'm Ashok Malhotra, an old fan of yours...". Most likely, Amitabh will acknowledge it gracefully and you may even ask for an autograph or a photograph with him, if you so desire.

In an office: You go to an office to meet Mr R.K. Sharma whom you have never met before. The best way is to walk up to the reception and enquire about him.

You: "Excuse me, I want to see Mr R.K. Sharma, the Assistant Sales Manager".

Receptionist: "May I know your name, please?"

You: "I'm Ashok Rana from Bharat Sales."

Receptionist: "Kindly wait, I'll inform him."

If there is no reception around, you can walk up to the first person you see and enquire: "Excuse me, I'm here to meet Mr R.K. Sharma. Would you be able to help me?"

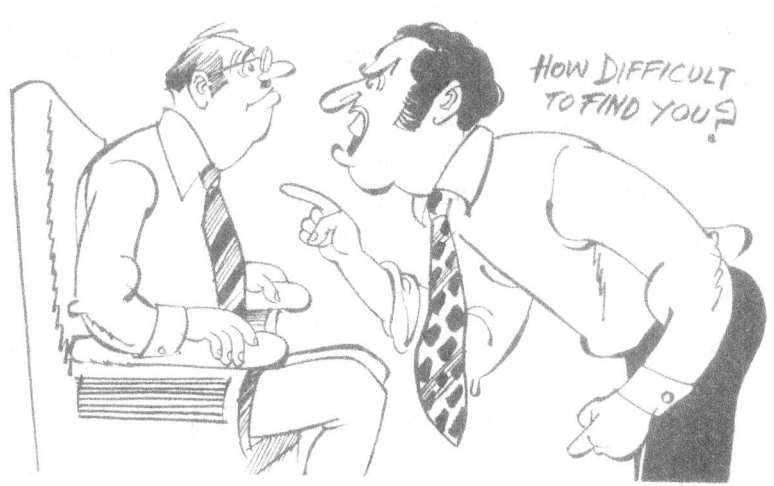

Reply: "You can go inside. He's in his office."

Once you have been able to locate Mr. Sharma's whereabouts, go up to him and introduce yourself.

You: "Mr Sharma?"

Mr Sharma: "Yes."

You: "Hello, I'm Ashok Rana from Bharat Sales...".

Come to the point right away. Don't start telling him how long it took you to locate him.

Introducing Children

When it comes to children, we find ourselves at a loss as to how to teach them to greet others. Children are shy and feel very self-conscious when introduced to others. Parents introduce their children to others in one of the following ways; Either the paretns will go on persuading the child (in front of the visitor) to greet the visitor (they can even be found threatening him like "I will not take you to the market if you do not say hello to Uncle") while the shy child would make every possible effort to bury his face in his mother's lap. In the other case, parents will leave the child out of introductions to the guests, ignoring him totally, not realizing that this may give the child an inferiority complex. Both these approaches are wrong. In the first case, the child is getting undesirable extra attention with the result that he becomes self-conscious and withdraws in his shell. In the second case, he is totally ignored. Since he has not been taught to greet people, he flounders. The child should be introduced to the visitor as a member of your family when the other introductions are being made. This not only makes him feel important, giving him an individual identity but at the same time gives him a sense of belonging.

Do not launch into a detailed description of his achievements, most recent activities, etc. Not only will this embarrass the child but bore the listeners.

As he sees others exchanging greetings, he imitates them. Try this a few times and you will never find him hiding behind a curtain whenever he is next called out to be introduced.

EXTENDING GREETINGS

'It dates back to the era of Cavemen.
Hands were extended to show that they were empty
a la handshake today.
With the only difference that it was a
sword in those times,
today it may be a remote control device
for that bomb planted under your seat.'

A smile is the most beautiful part of one's personality. You can make friends by a mere smile. And why not? Who wouldn't like to be friend a person with a smiling face? A smile exudes warmth. We greet our friends, relatives, acquaintances and superiors not only at the first meeting of the day but often repeatedly at brief intervals throughout the day. Thus, a smile creates and confirms the warmth in the relations without having to utter a word. It is a consent to friendly contact.

The manner in which persons greet each other varies from place to place. But greeting people at least the first time you see them each day is a polite custom. For the rest of the day, you can make do with a smile. Do not force yourself to smile as its artificiality is evident at once.

Often people are shy and they may be waiting for the other person to take the lead in greeting them. Well, there is no harm even if you are their superior. It will only enhance your image in their eyes. So always be prepared to intitiate a greeting. Because it is these little things in life that eventually blossom into lasting relationships. A warm greeting, besides breaking the veneer of formality, spells goodwill.

There are several forms of greeting — a friendly smile, a nod, a wink, a handshake, a kiss and most common in our surroundings — a *namaste*.

Verbal greetings

'Hello' is the universal verbal form of greeting which is acceptable in most situations — even strangers say Hello in passing. A more modern and popular usage is 'Hi'. Both these are said with a smile on the lips and a slight nod of head. A reply to these can either be a plain Hi or Hello or if you wish, you can use the added pleasantry "How are you"? It is often used as a gambit to start off the conversation.

Now starting a conversation does not necessarily mean that you should take the other person's words literally by reciting a long detailed list of your physical and mental ailments or your financial problems.

The response to "How are you?" should be "Fine, thank you, how are you?" and nothing more than this.

Shaking Hands

People shake hands more frequently today than they did years ago. Today, the handshake has come to be the most accepted form of greeting and occurs in the most varied cultural areas of the world with a few exceptions. The Japanese, for instance, do not shake hands; they bow and the depth of the bow is generally related to the degree of respect due to the person being greeted. In India,

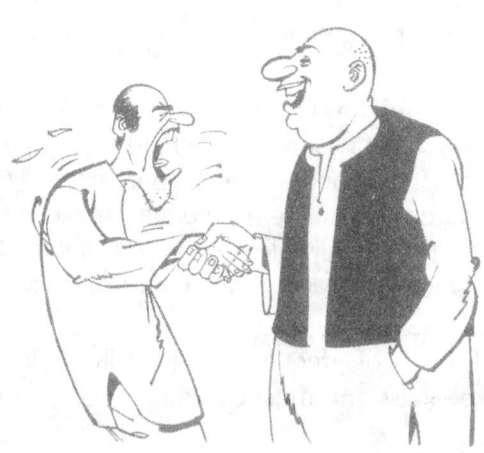

the traditional form of greeting elders is touching their feet and saying 'namaste' with folded hands. However, with modernization and the influx of western culture, these forms of greeting are not the rule everywhere.

There is more to a handshake than a flick of the wrist or the press of a palm. A handshake can reveal our hidden personality traits. Nobody likes a handshake that feels like a jellyfish or a vice-like grip that makes you wince. A firm but smooth grip is considered the best handshake. It gives a message of warmth and friendliness to the other person. In a sense, it seems to be saying: "You can depend upon me."

Handshaking usually accompanies all expressions of greeting, fare-wells, gratitude, congratulations, introductions, etc. When formally joining or departing from groups, it is customary to shake every individual's hands.

Namaste

Our country has the best answer to a greeting — the *namaste*. In large gatherings, one is saved the trouble of shaking (and experiencing) varied handshakes. The *namaste* symbolizes a welcome and reflects our traditional hospitality and service to others. And this is what makes it the most unique form of greeting in the world.

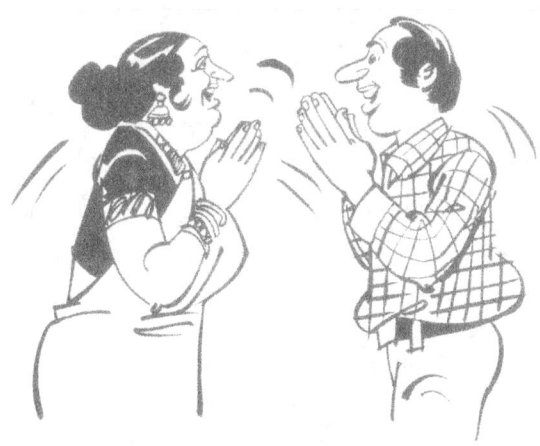

Some time back even *The Times* of London praised the *namaste* as a simple yet graceful and reticent Indian gesture of greeting. It further added, 'Today in Britain and elsewhere, by constantly wringing and kneading one another's hands during handshakes, many people worldwide often nurse sore thumbs and swollen wrists. In fact, many heads of state, politicians and even executives deliberately tone down the firmness of their otherwise warm handshakes. If only they could adopt and accept *Namaste* in place of handshake, we are sure they would be better off.'

Touching the Feet

This kind of greeting is only used by the young as a mark of respect to their elders. It is the traditional form of greeting in Indian culture.

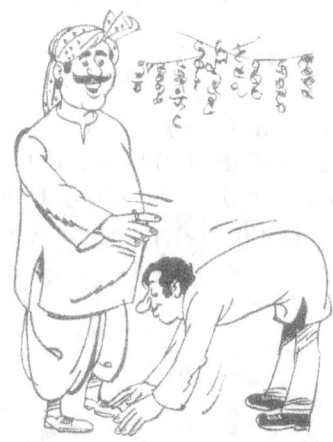

Young people bow down and touch the feet of their elders, who in turn bestow them with blessings like *'Jeete raho'*, *'Khush raho'*, etc.

Who would dare emulate the greeting of the *Masai* tribe of A rica?

On meeting one another, they spit and get spat back at!

Informal Greetings

This is the age of informal greetings and behaviour. But this does not mean that our friends should be greeted with thumps on their backs or subjected to nose-tweaking to signify our ready affection. It may instead keep them a mile away from you. If you want to exhibit your affection, a peck on the cheek should suffice. You may even resort to a friendly pat on the shoulder.

Greeting Someone on Entering

Men stand when they are introduced to each other. It is acceptable, however, for a woman to remain sitting when a man is presented to her. It is gracious to stand to greet anyone who comes into your house, office or any gathering with, of course, the exception of servants, co-workers or assistants who come in regularly.

Always stand to greet a visitor or when an exchange of handshakes or a namaste or maybe even a mere Hi-Hello takes place.

As soon as you have finished the greetings, invite the visitor to sit down and make himself comfortable.

How Children Should Greet their Elders

This is a question parents ask themselves when they begin teaching their child to greet others. Should the child be taught to say namaste, or hello; to shake hands or touch the feet? Since the child cannot differentiate between the variety of people you entertain, he must be properly guided.

Start with teaching him only one way of greeting. In a joint family, a boy can be taught to touch his elders' feet. However, in some families, as girls are not allowed to do this before marriage, they may be taught to say namaste.

If you are the type that entertains friends very often, your child may be taught to say a polite 'Hello'.

A child looks very sweet, shaking hands with the guests, but not every child is willing to do it, so instead of embarrassing yourself and torturing the poor little by repeatedly coaxing him to go and shake hands with the guests, just stick to a 'hello', which the child will find much safer and will conform to easily.

Leave-taking, Dismissing or Escorting Someone

Leave-taking is also a part and parcel of greetings. By a gracious leave-taking of the person we have met, we only succeed in strengthening the bonds of friendship for the future. One has to use one's discretion to judiciously round up a conversation and take leave of the other. 'Bye', 'See you', 'Till next time then', 'I shall take leave of you now', etc. are some standard accepted norms used when parting company.

You can dismiss someone by simply nodding or thanking them. If the other person is taking leave, stand up and escort him to the main door. Then greet him accordingly as you greeted him when he entered.

A handshake or 'Hi' or a simple 'Bye' or 'See you soon' will also suffice. Or you may prefer to say *namaste* or touch the person's feet (depending on your relationship). Do not forget to ask them to come again and to keep in touch.

Important visitors require red-carpet welcome. It is gracious to walk the person to his car or whatever mode of transport he has.

If you are expecting a person, do not make them wait for too long.

Similarly, in an office, never allow an important visitor to find his own way out alone. If your office is a maze of corridors, extend this courtesy to even the most ordinary visitors.

Making Enquiries

At some point of time or the other, all of us have felt the need for establishing contact with total strangers for making certain enquiries. It may be in an office, seeking information or on the road for directions.

Good manners demand that we greet a person before proceeding to make our request, at least with a genuine smile. And don't forget, a simple "Thank you" after your doubts have been cleared.

CONVERSATION—MIND THAT LANGUAGE

There is no point in using time that could be spent on the polo field speaking to some idiot with nothing to offer but the time of day. Get right to the point. You've got no time to talk about the weather.

'What do you do?'
'I'm in steel.'
'Is that steel as in 'stainless' or steal as in 'blind'?'
A quick follow-up is needed.
'How's your profit margin?'
'Around two million.'
'A year?'
'No, a week.'
Forget polo — now you can talk about the weather.

Unless you are remarkably eloquent, which few of us are, your manner of speech will not be a cause for comment. But if you speak poorly or mess around with your native language, this will indeed be noticed. Speaking is idiosyncratic. It is a reflection of learned patterns of talking and personality. Poor speech may grate on the ears of others but is tolerated by all but the very blunt and outspoken in polite society.

Speaking Skills
The first rule of speaking is: if you can't do it well, do something to remedy the situation. Take the help of 'Do-it-yourself' courses designed to help improve speech. Or get a friend to point out the errors of your speech. A good way to know whether you have a communication problem is observing your listeners reaction to you.

A long-winded person soon makes everyone in the room uncomfortable. Besides frequently being and often rudely interrupted, he is rarely listened to with close attention.

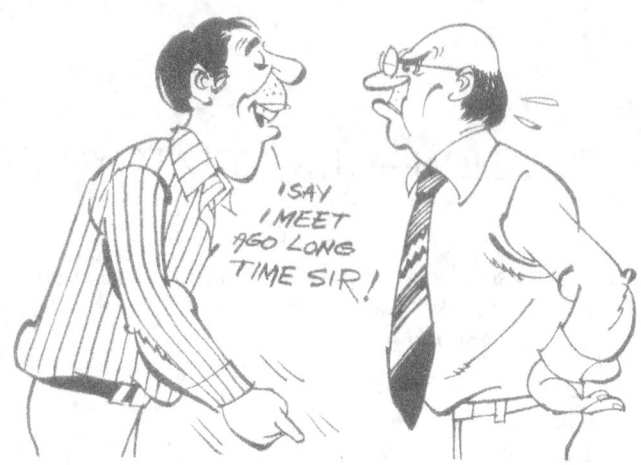

If you are talking too fast or too slow or in an accent that is hard to understand — your listeners may ask you to repeat something several times or tell you at a later point that they missed a part of what you had said earlier. These will give you indications that your speech delivery is somewhat erroneous. Poor grammar or misuse of a word is more difficult to detect since the polite refrain from reacting negatively to such errors. The only remedy for this problem is by listening to the speech of others and see how yours differs.

When analyzing the effect your spoken words have on others, if you find that you are getting more negative signals, take them as an indication that a little self-improvement is in order.

Listening

Listening to others is an art in itself and an integral part of etiquette. Listening is a supreme compliment to a speaker. It nevers fails to reap benefits for the listener. Focus your attention on the person who is speaking and do not interrupt. Look the speaker directly in the eye most of the time. Lean slightly forward if you are sitting to indicate interest. And if possible, sit close to the speaker.

Certain gestures of the listener reveal moments when their attention has been caught unequivocally. They may take off their glasses when the conversation takes a particularly fascinating turn or may lean forward in their chair as if not to miss a single word or cup their chin in their palm and fix unwavering attention and unblinking eyes on the speaker.

Above all, when you are listening to someone, do not look as if you are mentally planning what you want to say next. As a listener, you are expected to react to what you are hearing. Body language, nods or an emphatic shake of the head at appropriate moments reveal more than words. Slip in phrases like "I agree completely," or "You are absolutely right on that point", or "Quite true".

If you disagree with the point being made, you might say, "I'll have to give that some more thought," or even simply, "I'm not sure I agree with you on that point".

Perhaps the subtlest statement ever heard along these lines is, "You may be right". Spoken in just the right tone, this statement carries the silent implication, "But I doubt it".

Conversational Starters

Starting a conversation with your friends and acquaintances is not a hurdle. It is only when you are introduced to a stranger that you are at a temporary loss for words.

Let's assume that you've gone to a party and have just been introduced to a stranger. In such a situation, it is always desirable to initiate a conversation on a general topic. For example:

"Where are you working?"

"I'm with Hindustan Lever."

If you are familiar with any latest business happenings in that particular organization, you can expand further on these lines. If not, you can still go on to talk about safe and general topics like films, sports, politics, the weather, etc. For example:

"Have you been in Delhi long?" or

"Oh, it's so hot today!" or

"What a coincidence that you are also fond of gardening! That's my favourite pastime too."

If it is an intimate gathering where people know each other well, any topic under the sun may be broached. But keep in mind that whatever you talk of must be of interest to everyone. Jokes and anecdotes come quite handy at such occasions. Try to refrain from talking shop. This can only be of interest when it is an interdepartment office party. Not when there is only a handful of people from the same organization or line of profession present in the group.

If it is a courtesy visit you are paying to your grandparents or uncles, aunts or some other elderly family friends, the conversation automatically follows an altogether different pattern. As you belong to a different age and era, your elderly relations have fixed opinions about certain things. It is better to let them do most of the talking, usually starting with a 'In our days...'. Don't let it bother you. Just remember, the time when you hark back to 'your' days is not very far either.

Even if you disagree on certain points, it is disrespectful to criticize old people. Even though you know they are wrong, do not try to urge your point home and give cause for offence. It is safer to ostensibly agree with them.

Using Flattery Wisely

There is an art to flattering someone. Flattery can be done in two ways:

(a) To compliment excessively and often insincerely, especially in order to win the favour of someone.

(b) To portray someone favourably.

When going about the business of flattering someone, make very sure that you follow the second mode. False flattery rarely sounds like anything but what it is.

Another commonly followed mode of flattery is by complimenting a person. You like the tie someone is wearing, and you tell him so simply and briefly. A colleague is carrying an especially handsome leather purse; again, you tell her so pleasantly and briefly. These little compliments on another's tastes not only makes them feel good, but also puts you in their good books forever. You just have to be a little careful not to overdo the amount of flattery and to continue sounding authentic.

A more intensive form of flattery should still be honest, while having a definite motive.

If, for example, your friend wrote a good article which has been published in *The Times of India,* do not say: "That article you wrote was really dynamite. Just marvelous. How do you do it?"

Instead, with a little thought, something better and more realistic like this can be said "Your article in *The TOI* was very impressive. Especially that point you made about future developments." With this compliment, you have shown your appreciation of the article and reflection on it.

Avoiding Slang

Slang is often used when talking with your peer group. Your elders and other family friends and superiors in your place of work should be given the respect due to them by keeping slang out of your speech.

Slang often displays a sense of belonging — to define who is out and who is in — specially at the college level. Taken to extremes, this is rude behaviour. Remember abusive and swear slang vocabulary should not be a part of a ladies' conversation. Even when in a temper, keep your tongue under control.

Art of Conversation and Your Child

It is very important to inculcate the art of conversation in children. They learn a lot by observing. How you converse with others is keenly observed by your little one and then imitated to the letter.

For a child, the first rule for a good conversation should be politeness and respect to others. Be it elders or his peer group, he should be taught the correct manner of speech.

Slang should be kept out of 'polite' conversation. Keep a watch out for any use of swear words or cursing in your child's speech. An immediate stop should be put to bad language.

They should also be taught not to intervene while two persons are talking. They should wait for them to finish before saying what he has to. Polite words like, Please, Thank you, Excuse me, Bye, Hello, How do you do, Sorry, etc. should be made an essential part of his speech and he should use them frequently and appropriately.

Sarcasm, Humour, Double Meanings

The above three in a conversation can be destructive if misused. Don't make uncalled-for wisecracks at a gathering or party unless you know the people very well and know that your comments will not be taken amiss. Refrain from double-edged ambiguous statements and keep your sarcasm and deadly wit for intimate gatherings.

Dirty jokes must be taken out of the closet only when two or three good friends are together and that too only in male company. Men should not insult the presence of a lady by relating vulgar jokes. A lady on the other hand should not give rise to unsavoury gossip by telling these jokes herself. There are many funny jokes that can be said without being crude or vulgar.

Modulating Your Voice

Modulation refers to the rhythm and tonal quality of your voice. It is specially important not to talk too loudly. If you are at an intimate romantic lunch, it would be embarassing if the whole restaurant got to know your boyfriend has just proposed to you.

On the other hand, a voice that is too soft and can barely be heard will fail to make an impact of any sort. In fact, an extremely soft voice can make one appear weak and ineffective.

So all those who want to be respected and listened to should make an effort to maintain a well-modulated voice most of the time. Also make sure that your voice, while being pleasant, is loud enough to be understood.

Filling Those Gaps

A good conversationalist does not dominate a conversation but permits others to have their say as well. But at times, there may be such gaps in between the conversation when one doesn't know what to do and what to say. Pitch in when conversation begins to flag or trails to a halt. Subtle approaches are always best. A change of topic often helps in filling those gaps. So does calling a person's attention to what had been said earlier.

Accepting Criticism Graciously

Fault-finding and criticism is an irritating trait in many people. They delight in tearing others to pieces. No doubt, at times some people need and deserve criticism, but it should be done mildly and above all, constructively. Just telling somebody he is stupid, dumb and is doing something wrong not only turns that person into your biggest enemy but also demoralizes him. So be liberal in your encouragement. Instead, let the person know you have faith in his ability, that he has an untapped flair for it. The odds are he will put in his optimum effort in order to excel and please you.

Similarly, if you ever find yourself criticized, do not take it to heart. Take it in good faith and try to locate your fault and rectify it.

In fact, it is always better to keep criticism out of the general conversation. Instead, call a person aside and say what you have to privately.

Practising — A Final Word

Finally, the key to improving your speaking skills is practice. Watch others, and when you hear something that appeals to you, some phrase you think will work for you — adopt it in your speech.

It is true that poised speech is a sign of good manners and is one of the graces that anyone can acquire without too much effort.

MANAGING RELATIONSHIPS

Some of the ground rules in life may have changed in today's fast world but good manners have held their place. Getting to know the other person and managing relationships still holds an important place in our lives.

*R*elating to one's peers and others one may come in contact with is not easy today. There are three basic spheres in which you must learn to co-exist with your peers and there is an etiquette to each sphere.

First of all, you should learn to be a gracious gentleman or lady. Second, you must know how to handle sticky situations with tact and delicacy. Thirdly, it is important to show good manners and appreciation in all your dealings with people.

Discourtesy

Discourtesy is when you clearly insult someone. It is mostly intentional but at times a person not too well versed with the rules of manners and etiquette may behave in a fashion that is considered discourteous by others. Such as by not getting up from your seat when the boss enters your cabin, or not saying 'Thank you' when someone has served you a dish. Discourtesy is the biggest enemy of relationships. If you are not on the same wavelength as the other person, a slight error or discourtesy in behaviour on your part may prove fatal to the bond you could have developed later.

Relationships with Friends

'Whoever finds a friend finds a treasure' — cherish friendship so it can be treasured forever. Always be polite and helpful. Your friend should be proud to be your friend. This requires a lot of mutual effort — from your side and of course, from your friends' side as well.

If you are going for a picnic or lunch date, go dutch and share equal responsibility of arrangements and finances.

If you often extend monetary help to each other, keep a record of it and never forget to pay back whatever you owe . Since money is the root of all major disputes, be extra careful.

Do not be possessive. You are not that person's only friend and should not even attempt to be. A jealous friend destroys a relationship and these misunderstandings can ruin your relations with even your best friend.

Also, never take your friend for granted. You have to make constant efforts to nourish a friendship and to keep it going smoothly. On the other hand, remember that familiarity breeds contempt. Give one another breathing space. Prying into anyone's family affairs is not a good practice — even if it is your best friend. Unless, of course, he himself is willing to talk about it, don't probe. Even if he does tell you a secret, keep it to yourself.

Don't try to patronize him. You might lose him in the bargain. Always treat him with consideration and care. Learn to respect his feelings and be sensitive to his moods.

Your Neighbours

You have recently moved into a new house and want to establish cordial relations with your neighbours. You call on them and in no time pave the grounds for friendship. You find out that she is addicted to gossip. With her children away at hostel and husband at work, she has plenty of free time on her hands — which unfortunately you do not have. Still you enjoy the gossip and spend a great deal of time with her either in your house or at hers. But in your newfound hobby (gossip), you forget how shabby your living room has started to look or your lagging correspondence or how much your husband is missing his daily hot snack on his return from work. On the other hand your neighbour is enjoying the benefits of your imported mixie, bone-china tea set, beautifully embroidered table cloths and your culinary abilities by making you cook special dishes. Once your enthusiasm for gossip wears off, you start resenting her. To top it all, she uses your phone to chat with her friends and mother.

Don't be too isolated either. Neighbours are the first people to call on when in trouble at home. A neighbourly relationship is very tricky. If you play your cards right, you may end up with a good and helpful friend, but if you overdo it, it may become a liability after some time. It is safest to keep your distance without being rude. Exchange greetings and a few words every day but don't let the two households merge! If you lose your privacy, it is difficult to get it back.

Servants/Assistants

There is a vast difference of status between an assistant and a servant. The assistant definitely calls for better treatment than your daily help. An assistant can be anybody from a compounder to a doctor, a personal secretary in an office to a housekeeper at home. Be open and friendly without actually being friends. Don't constantly remind them that they are your inferiors. Especially a governess or tutor for your children. If the older members of the family show proper respect to them, children will also emulate this behaviour. However, that doesn't mean that you can entrust them with the house keys or make them your confidant. A clear line of demarcation should always be there — treat them well but not intimately.

Servants have to be handled with kid gloves. Instead of shouting and abusing them, insist on showing them who's the boss right from the start. They should be given orders politely but firmly. If they have committed a mistake, shouting will get you nowhere. Deal with the situation sensibly and quietly and tell them not to repeat it again. However, if incompetence is a daily affair, get new help. Never show them how dependent on them you are.

Teacher-Student Relationship

The *guru-shishya* relationship dates centuries back. This relationship calls for a lot of caution and care. While on the one hand, a teacher is a model for the students, the students must extend proper respect to their teachers. To understand each other better, the teacher should try to see things from the student's point of view. A wrongdoer should not be judged too harshly. Explain to him where

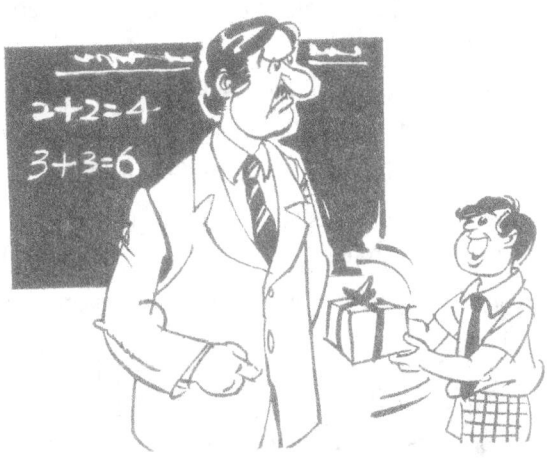

exactly and how he has erred and emphasize the need to amend his ways. Punishment should be at the minimum, and that too not very harsh. Every class has some intelligent students and some not-too-bright. Do not discriminate between the two. Treating students as personal flunkeys or asking the students of influential parents for favours portrays a bad image of a teacher. Such a teacher can never win the students' respect.

On the other hand, students must give teachers their due respect. Listen attentively in class and don't distract others by laughing sense-lessly or talking. Making fun of teachers may make you popular among your fellow students for a short while. Don't try to bribe your teacher with expensive gifts, etc. Fresh flowers, good conduct and the respect shown to the teacher is enough to keep up a good relationship going with your her/him.

Customer-Shopkeeper Relationship

This can be likened to a waiter-customer relationship in a restaurant. Do not make the mistake (if you are a customer) of expecting to be waited upon hand on foot. The shop assistant or waiter is not your personal servant. He is there to cater to your needs, among a host of other people, who have as many demands as you.

If you are a customer: Avoid going to a shop from where you don't actually intend buying anything. Be sure about what you want to buy — don't just aimlessly see this or that and waste the shopkeeper's time.

Do not shop in a large group. Too many people loitering in a shop are apt to put off other customers who think it is too crowded.

Do not haggle where it is not an accepted practice.

Do not be rude, terse or abusive. Put yourself in his place — what is the kind of behaviour that you would expect from a customer?

If you are a shopkeeper: Always greet your customer with a smile. Be prompt in attending to them. Even if they leave without buying anything, don't lose your temper. They do have a right to look around the market. If the customer forgets something behind at the shop, keep it in safe custody till he comes back to claim it. An honest person is appreciated.

Try to be accommodative should the customer wish to exchange an item bought earlier.

Parent-Child Relationship

This is one of the most important relationships in life. To a parent, a child is the centre of his world — the same applies to children. Children are at the learning stage, besides observing your behaviour, attitude and ways of dealing with them and others very closely. Refrain from double standards. For example, if you teach him one day that lying is wrong and the next day, you make him answer the door and tell so-and-so person that you are not at home, this discrepancy will confuse him. Until he/she is of the age to understand the difference between white lies and the wrong ones, practice what you preach.

Be a ready listener and listen patiently. Do not hush him up every time he opens his mouth to say something, no matter what he may interrupt. It is very important for him to be able to communicate with you. This not only helps him become articulate and more outgoing but also establishes a healthy relationship between you two. By getting your undivided attention, he gets assured that you care.

If you are the proud parents of more than one child, share your love equally among them. Do not lavish attention on the brightest or your favourite and make the others feel inferior in any way. Treat them as separate individuals yet members of the same family. Never make the mistake of comparing them. Instead, encourage their respective qualities and watch them grow with love and affection. Your relationship with your child will be reflected in his behaviour in later years. If you play your cards right today, you will be amply rewarded by a sincere, loving, caring, long-lasting relationship for life.

GOING STEADY

A word of odim to the girls: don't appear too anxious, or even anxious at all. Play indeed hard to get.

"I am sorry. I wasn't listening. What did you say?"
"Would you like to go out for dinner?"
"Oh, who is this nice looking fellow here with you?"
"I'm asking you for dinner!"
He is a gentleman but ignore it.
"Um... let's see. But what's his name?"
"He's John. Now how about tonight?"
"Oh well, if you insist."
"Whippie!"
"With him, silly, not with you!"

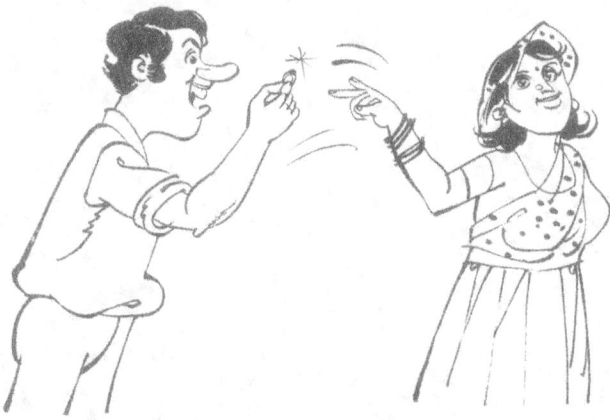

*I*n the complicated yet delicate task of establishing a relationship with a member of the opposite sex, knowing how to behave courteously will assist you in awkward situations and be a guide in difficult situations.

Young men and women now enjoy an independence unrivalled in the social history of this country. Earlier, marriage between a boy/girl belonging to the same community, religion, caste, and social strata was decided upon by the parents — both families decided which couple would be compatible and therefore suited to being life partners. This was the custom but changing times and our permissive society are bringing about sweeping changes.

Meeting Each Other

With more and more co-ed schools, the chances of boys and girls meeting have increased. Since they do meet in school and are classmates, the next step is for them to meet socially.

Parties

Teenage parties are seldom an all-girl or all-boy affair. Both sexes do mingle and these parties should be under the chaperonage of at least one responsible adult. Organize interesting games which will set the mood of the party.

Dancing

Dancing may be allowed for a while. Normally, the boy asks the girl of his choice to dance, "May I have this dance, please?" or "May I have the pleasure of being your partner for this dance?" Do not walk up to her and jerk your thumb in the direction of the dance floor lifting one eyebrow in query.

It is the girl's prerogative to refuse a dance but at house parties where everyone is known to each other, it is rude to refuse to dance. If, however, you have a reason, then do say as much to the boy who has asked you to dance. "I'd love to but I'm afraid the heel of my shoe just broke", and laughingly show it to him. Or you could say, "The music is rock and roll and I'm not a good jiver or twister so I hope you don't mind if I sit this one out".

Dates

Asking her out: The next step from here would be to go out together. A boy may approach a girl and invite her out for a movie, or if he can escort her to a party, or have lunch with him. A straightforward approach should be adopted. Do not ask a girl vaguely: "What are you doing this Saturday?" Instead, ask her frankly "Would you like to go to a movie this Saturday?", stating a good film that is showing at a theatre.

Refusing a date: A girl has the option of accepting or refusing a date. In case she does not wish to meet the boy she should firmly but politely be brief and round up the conversation. In case she is interested but cannot accept the date due to some prior engagement she may mention the nature of the engagement, adding 'Perhaps if it's still running next Saturday?"

If you as a girl are not allowed to date, tell the boy you can only be friends with him.

On a Date

Boys: When dating a girl after meeting her at the appointed place and time don't say "What do we now?". Have the outing planned out in keeping with your budget, even book the movie tickets in advance.

Do not tell her crude jokes more suited for your all-boy gang.

Do not try to hold hands or paw her on the first few dates.

Do not drink or press her to do the same.

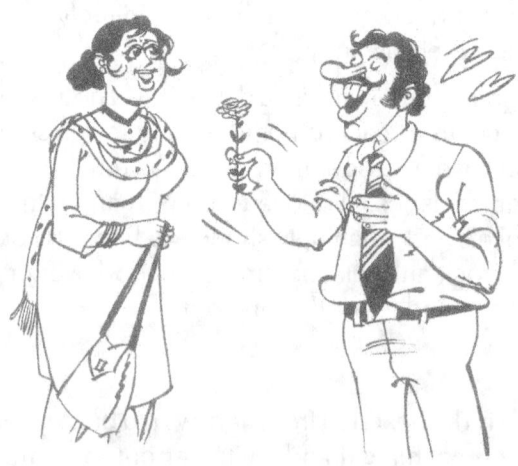

Girls: If your date takes you to a place which is not to your liking or you feel the movie is not suitable for teenagers, politely state your feelings. Put him in his place at once if he crosses limits and tries to paw you. Do not accept gifts from your date. A bunch of flowers, however is acceptable.

Dropping the Date Home

The boy is expected to see the girl home but need not be invited inside. After a few dates, it may be okay. Actually, some girls do introduce their dates to their parents before going out with them. It depends upon you and your parents. If the boy picks a girl up from her home instead of meeting at a predetermined place, she may introduce him to her parents.

Compliments

Many people find accepting personal compliments an awkward ordeal. Refrain from analysing a compliment and holding it up to see if it is sincere and honest. It is a verbal gesture and should be accepted as such. The recipient may smile enigmatically and say nothing, or look pleased, or simply respond with a warm Thank you. Some may even parry the remark with a laugh or shrug their shoulders.

Boy: "Rita, what beautiful hair you have."

Girl: "Thanks to Lakme, it's looking its best these days — all the same, thanks Jai."

Or:

Jai: "Rita, what beautiful hair you have!"

Rita: "Thanks, Jai, even I pride myself on it."

Never react like this:

Rita: "What nonsense — my hair is very dull, so forget the compliments, buddy."

This is extremely rude and discourteous.

Teenagers, don't forget this is the age of friendship. Go out on dates, enjoy yourselves with good clean fun, but don't let mistakes of youth mar a bright future. There's plenty of time for serious romance, affairs and marriage. Remember to take your parents into confidence. They are the best friends you can ever have and want the best for you.

If they prefer that you do not go out alone with a boy, then you can have as much fun with your peers at picnics, get-togethers, house parties, etc. where both the sexes are invited.

YOU AND FOOD

"Dinner is served!"
The cry emanates from a butler standing at the doorway
to where food is being served. It is the signal for you to
stop whatever you're doing or saying, and rush to the
grub before it gets cold.

"Table Manners"? You may scoff and say, "are they important? After all, don't education, skills, contacts and personality count more? I have all this and more." True, but these pale into
insignificance if your eating habits and table manners make you
look ridiculous. There's no point in being well-dressed, conversant,
and polite if at the table you spill food around your plate, stretch
out in front of your neighbour to reach for a particular dish, in the
process knocking over his glass of water, chew your food noisily,
slurp loudly, wipe your fingers on the table-cloth, waste food... Need
I go on?

To someone who has been taught correct manners right from the
cradle, good table manners are second nature. It is these persons
who notice how others eat. Remember that lack of table manners is
simply an indication of your level of sophistication, your upbringing
and on the whole puts you in a poor perspective.

Fortunately, while some other aspects of manners are linked to
personal qualities, table manners can be inculcated by anyone.
No one is born with them. If you offend others' sensibilities — like
putting used cutlery on the table, talking with your mouth full, or
waving your fork around — then your table manners, or lack of
them, are noticed. Many of the strict stipulations of as recent as a
decade ago have by now vanished. For example, these days it is not
particularly important to open a dinner-sized napkin halfway and
luncheon napkin all the way. What is important is remembering to
put the open napkin in your lap.

Table Settings

Formal: The first requisite of good table manners is to become familiar with the the table settings, particularly in restaurants where meals are served in courses, i.e. various dishes are brought to the table in a sequence and different plates, silverware and glassware are used for each course.

Three course dinners are usually served on formal occasions today. At even the most formal dinner, you will not be confronted with more than three forks, possibly two spoons and two knives at the side of your place. If any more silverware is required, it will be brought in with various courses.

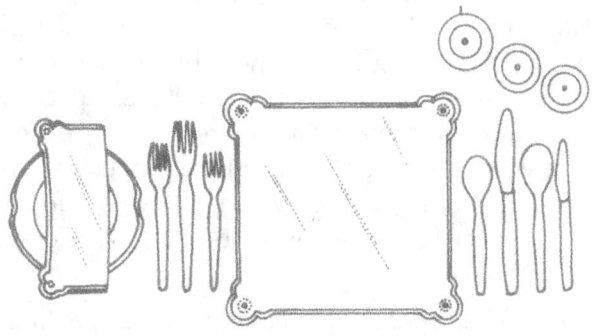

An example of a formal place setting with dessert spoon and fork set upright on either side.

An easy rule governs the order in which the forks and knives are to be used. Start from the outside and work your way inwards. This means you start with the first fork or spoon on the outside of the setting and use each consecutive piece of silverware as each course is served. There is usually a different spoon for soup, and one for rice. The fish knife is different from the butter knife and so is the knife to be used when cutting food into edible pieces.

Informal: In an informal setup, say at a friend's or relative's house, usually just one spoon, fork and knife are used. The knife may or may not be present. If soup is there, a separate soup spoon is kept alongside the dinner spoon.

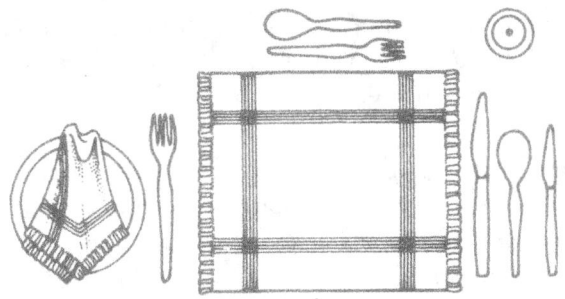

An example of an informally arranged place setting with dessert spoon and fork set horizontally across the top.

The fork here is held in the left hand and spoon in the right. The spoon is used for putting food in your mouth and fork there to help in putting the food into the spoon.

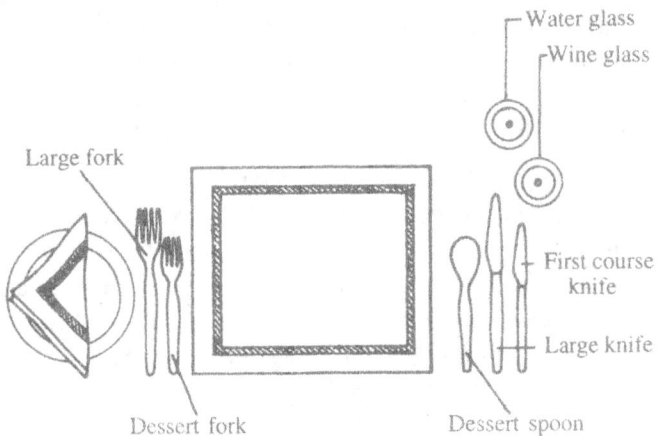

An example of a place setting for a three course lunch or dinner.

At home: Most traditional Indian homes have their meals in a *thali*. A big steel *thali* (almost double than the usual dinner plate) is placed in front of the diner with several small steel bowls (*katoris*) for dal, curry, curds, etc. Spoons are used for serving the food which is generally eaten with fingers.

However, if you prefer a dinner-size plate to a *thali*, all the accessories remaining same, the big *thali* is substituted by a smaller steel plate. Occasionally, a fork may also be present, but it varies from each individual to another. You use what you find most convenient and are comfortable using.

Teaching Your Child

In some communities, the first grain of rice that a child eats is an occasion for celebration. To inculcate good eating habits in your child, it is very important that you observe these golden rules at home regularly.

Teach the child gently yet firmly all that he should gradually know. Do not scold a child when he spills food over his plate. Be patient with him and teach him the basics as a first round. Do not go into all the details at once. A practical method of teaching is always better. If you go on telling him how to do this or that, do not expect a child to put it into practice flawlessly. Seat him besides yourself when you are eating and show him what to do. Even after you have demonstrated a few table manners to him, do not expect miracles in the first instance. He must do it himself and practise regularly. You are very much at fault if you expect your child to be an expert on table manners after just a couple of lectures on the subject.

Yours may be a household where you eat with your hands. Definitely, the child must learn to eat adeptly with his hands without making a mess of his face, hands and the area around his plate. But do not forget to teach him the use of a spoon, fork and knife also. Or else, when he goes out and is expected to use them, he will be at a total loss. So, remember, practice is the keyword. Give him lots of practice and see how quickly he learns.

Eating Implements

Using a fork and spoon: The combination of a fork and spoon is very common. The fork is held in the left hand and is used to hold a piece of vegetable or meat to be cut with a knife. It is also used to provide support to a spoon.

Using a spoon only: If you wish to use only the spoon, then gravy dishes, *dal*, curd and rice etc. can be eaten easily with it. For non-

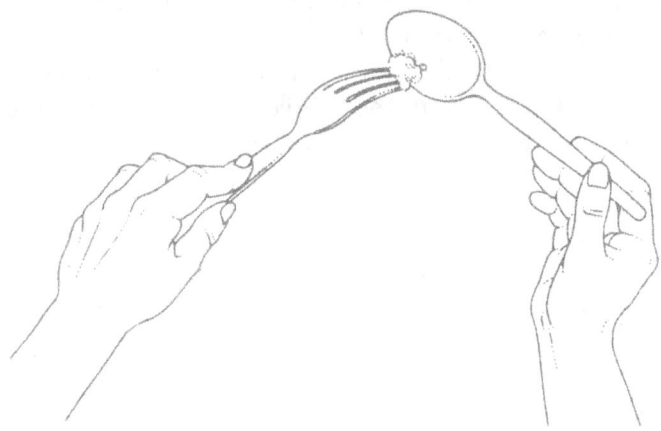

Holding a spoon and fork

vegetarian dishes, especially the boned pieces of chicken or mutton, you will have to use your hands, or a knife and fork. Two pieces of cutlery are usually used at a sit-down meal. At a garden party or a buffet, usually one uses either a spoon or a fork as one hand is used to hold your plate.

Using a fork only: By transferring the fork to the right hand, it may be used as a spoon with the prongs facing upwards. The upper part of the handle is held between the index and middle fingers just like a spoon, and thumb is used to hold the fork steady. The fourth and little fingers are closed together in support of the fingers gripping the handle.

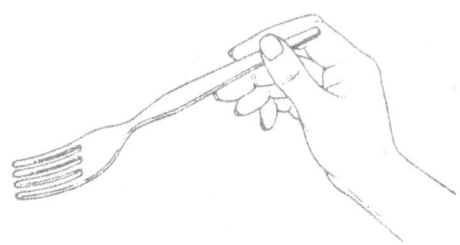

Holding a fork

Holding a knife and fork: When a fork is used with a knife, it is held in the left hand and the prongs face downwards. The handle of the knife is held with the end covered by the palm and the index finger resting on the length. The handle is supported by the thumb on one side and the remaining fingers on the other side.

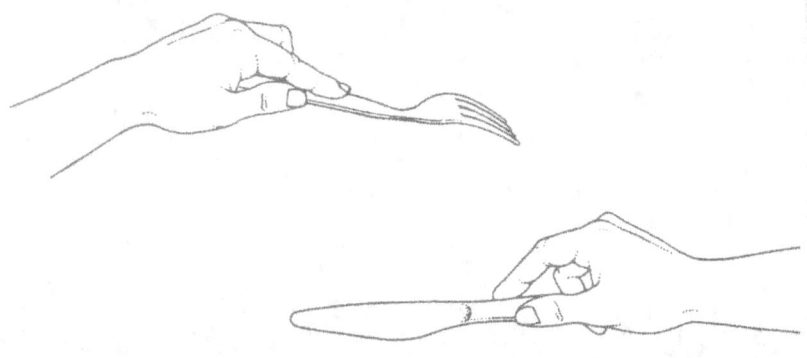

Using a fork and knife

This method ensures a good grip and helps to prevent the sharp edge of the knife's blade from slipping dangerously backward and also enables the diner to keep his elbows to his sides, instead of them digging into the ribs of his neighbour.

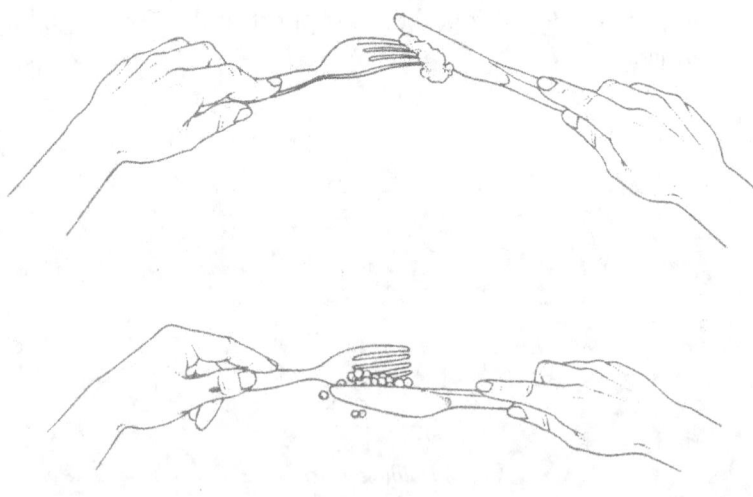

Cutting up food on your plate is delicate business. However much you may like to chop your entire portion into small pieces before starting to eat, refrain from doing so as it is not the done thing. Cut one piece at a time, eat it and then repeat the process. Similarly, in the case of *paranthas* — you tear a small piece, eat it and then repeat the process. Have you ever seen a person divide a *chapati* or *roti* into tiny bits and then eat them? A knife is also used for pushing — the width of the blade helps to push food onto the back of the fork.

Using chopsticks: The popularity of Chinese dishes has led to the widespread use of chopsticks. Although they are not very common in India, one should still know how they are to be used. It is mainly learned through practice. Use the thumb and index fingers to hold both the sticks. The remaining fingers should give support. With the help of the thumb, place the two sticks apart, while the index finger should be free to be used as a lever. Pick up the food with the help of the sticks and tighten the grip of the sticks on the food by moving the top chopsticks with the help of the index finger accordingly. Now push the food into your mouth.

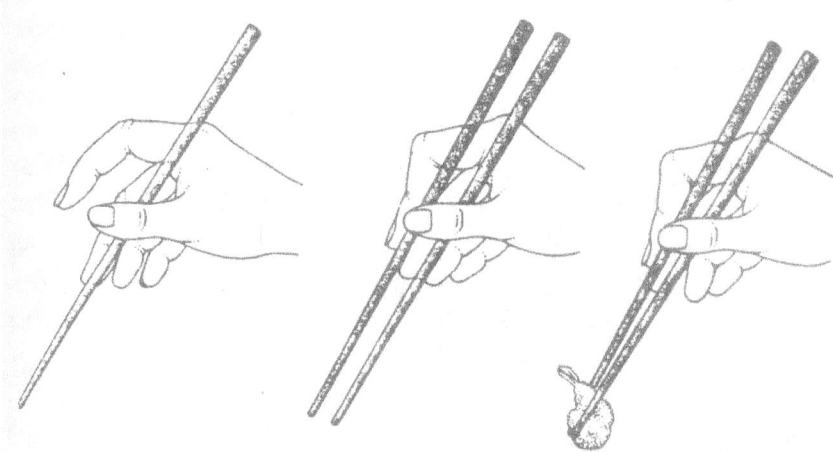

Holding chopsticks

Eating with chopsticks is fun. It is said that the Chinese themselves invented the fork but after some time went back to their original and more practical way of eating with chopsticks.

Continental Food

When eating continental food, say steak or *pasta*, the fork is held in the left hand, and the knife in the right hand throughout the meal. The food is pushed onto the fork by a slight nudge with the side of the knife. Once firmly on the fork, the food is transferred to the mouth. Between mouthfuls, don't wave your cutlery in the air or point it at a person to emphasize a point. If you must speak when eating, wait till you have swallowed your mouthful, put down your spoon and fork and then speak.

Indian Style

We may claim to have become modern and westernized but at heart and habits we are still Indian. Indian eating habits do not demand the strict use of knife or fork or even spoon. We prefer to rely upon our God-given five fingers. However, spoons are most commonly used. We eat almost everything with a spoon. Forks are used to help out.

The Courses

Meals at home are not usually served in courses. However, a meal may be broadly divided as such:

Course 1   — An appetizer like *jaljira*; or light *pakoras*.

Course II   — This is the main meal consisting of a *dal* dish, vegetable dishes, curd, *chaptai*, rice, *papad*, *chatni*, etc. or meat.

Course III   — In some communities there is another course before the dessert, which may be *papad* or curd-rice, etc.

Course IV   — Is the dessert.

Northern India

The food eaten in northern parts of India consists of both rice and wheat dishes. A dish of lentil is eaten with rice along with some vegetable dishes and *chapatis* made of wheat flour. The meal starts with the serving of *dal* and vegetables and curd in the neatly placed *katoris*. *Papad*, *chatni* and salad are additional savouries. Then hot *chapatis* are served one by one. Once the diner is through with the *chapatis*, rice is served. Both *chapatis* and rice are eaten with *dal*, vegetables and curd simultaneously.

In the Marwari and Sindhi communities, the *papad* is not served with the main meal, but after the meal is over. In fact, it is an indication that the meal is over. And finally, a dessert which can either be served in the beginning along with the other food items or separately after the main course.

There is no strict rule as to when and what to eat. You only eat whatever is served, as and when, in the *thali*. If a spoon is there in the *thali*, use it, otherwise rely on your fingers.

Southern India

The staple food of southern India is rice. When thinking of southern cuisine, it is the *idli, dosa* and *uttapams,* that come readily to the mind. Little do we know that there is much more it than just these.

At a formal south Indian meal, *idlis* or *dosas* are never served as the main meal. In most of the traditional south Indian gatherings, especially weddings, plantain leaves are preferred, even today, to a *thali*. This huge leaf is placed in front of the guest. One by one, each dish is served on the leaf. Until all the items are served, the diner does not start eating. The curry and the vegetable dishes are served on the outer side of the leaf whereas rice in the middle of the leaf. The serving is done from the right to left of the leaf.

A formal south Indian meal consists of two lentil dishes – the *rasam* and the *sambhar* – three or four vegetable dishes, one curd, curd-rice and one dessert and *papad, chatni,* etc. follow suit.

The diner tastes each dish separately by mixing it with rice; quite unlike the north-Indian diner who is allowed to mix everything together – if he so desires – and enjoy himself. Eating in south India is also done the same way as it is served, i.e. from the right to left.

Food on plantain leaves is always eaten with the fingers. No spoons are provided to the diner.

Eastern India

Usually, big *thalis* are used for eating food. If *katoris* are there for the curries etc., they are all placed inside the *thali* and all the other items except for rice are served in them. Rice, which is the main dish, is served in the middle of the *thali*. There it is divided into various portions by the diner and eaten separately with the different items of *dal*, curries, fish curry, etc. which may be served. In this style of eating, as soon as the first curry is put on the first portion of rice, the diner starts eating. The next curry is only put on the second portion of rice after the first portion is finished, and so on. Finally, the dessert.

Western India

It is is quite similar to the north Indian style. Although the method of preparating of dishes is different from theirs, the ways of serving and eating are quite similar.

How to Eat Various Dishes

SOUTH INDIAN CUISINE

Dosa/uttapam: A *dosa* or an *uttapam* is eaten with the fingers. If you prefer not to, you may use a knife and a fork. With a knife in your right hand and fork in the left. The knife is used for cutting pieces and fork for putting them in the mouth. The pieces are cut one by one and eaten simultaeously at the same time with coconut *chatni* and *sambhar*.

Idly/vada: *Idly* and *vada* are eaten with a spoon or if at home, then with the fingers. The practice of first soaking them in *sambhar* and then eating them is wrong. In certain hotels where *sambhar* is provided in wide-mouthed bowls, you can soak the *idly* and *vada* in it. The correct way is to break off pieces with the spoon and eat them, then take a spoonful of the *sambhar*. The method of dipping the *idly/vada* piece in *sambhar* before putting it in your mouth is merely a shortcut.

Rice : The south Indian style of eating rice with fingers may not go too well in a posh restaurant. So choose a spoon, not a fork, because of the gravy dishes. However, a fork can be used as a support for pushing rice onto the spoon.

Besi bela huli anna: Many people may not be familiar with this dish. It is basically a rice dish in which a layer of rice and *dal* is covered with *sambhar*, vegetable and lots of dry fruits. It is eaten with a fork mixing everything together.

Papad: These are eaten with the hands after breaking the papad into small pieces.

NORTH INDIAN CUISINE
Chapati/puri/parantha: All these are eaten with the hands.

Vegetables: They are best eaten with *chapati/nan/puri*, etc. Dry vegetables are eaten with a fork. You may eat the curried versions with a spoon.

Koftas and curries: With the help of a fork, the *kofta* is broken into two or three pieces. Then either pick up each piece with a piece of *chaptai* or mix it with rice with the help of the same fork.

Kebabs and tikkas: They are best eaten with the hands. If you do not like to dirty your hands, eat them with a fork.

CHICKEN
With bone: A chicken can either be eaten with fingers or a knife and fork. Be careful not to stab at the chicken too hard as it may slip out of your plate, especially a greasy or curried one. It is perfectly okay to pick up a bone with your fingers.

Boneless: Pieces of chicken can be picked up on the fork and eaten as it is. If the piece is too big, take a bite from the side, putting the fork down between bites.

Tandoori: A *tandoori* chicken is eaten much in the same way as the chicken (with bones) and preferably with fingers.

Fish: Fried fish is eaten with a fork and knife which is used for cutting. If it is a big piece with bones, use a knife and fork to shred it and eat with the fork. Fish curry and rice taken at home is eaten with the fingers.

CHINESE
The use of chopsticks has already been discussed. This is a popular way of eating Chinese food without having to bother about forks, knives and spoons (except soup, of course), provided you know how to use the chopsticks.

Spring rolls: Either pick them up with chopsticks and eat them piece by piece or cut them bit by bit with a knife and fork. However, you can even pick it up in your hand and eat — the rules are not so strict today.

Chowmein/chopsuey/fried rice: Without chopsticks, the only way to eat chowmein and chopsuey is with a fork in your right hand. The long strands of noodle should be twirled around the prongs of the fork to make it easy to put them in your mouth.

Boneless chilli chicken: Either pick up the pieces between chopsticks and eat, otherwise it is eaten the same way as any other boneless chicken.

SNACKS

Burgers/hotdogs: Burgers and hotdogs can only be picked up using both your hands and then eaten. Don't feel awkward doing so.

Cutlets: Use a fork and knife for eating cutlets. The sauce may be poured on top of the cutlet or if kept at the side of the plate, dip a piece of the cutlet into it.

Pizzas: These are best eaten by picking up each slice in your fingers or a fork. The fork may be used for cutting as well as eating. The sauce, mustard, vinegar, etc. can be put on top of the toppings separately.

Pao bhaji: As the name suggests, it is a dish containing one vegetable dish and bread and may be eaten with your hands. Otherwise, use a fork and knife to cut the bread, and spoon to push the vegetables in your mouth.

Finger chips: Either pick up each chip, dip it in sauce and eat it or pour the sauce on top of the chips and eat them with a fork — both are correct, depending upon which way you are more comfortable with.

Omelette: If you are eating an omelette with bread slices, use a knife and fork. If an omelette by itself, use the fork alone.

Sandwiches: You cannot eat a sandwich with a fork or spoon, so just pick up a sandwich and munch on it.

Soup: The important rule to remember when drinking soup is not to slurp.

An occasional sound may be unavoidable but constant slurping tends to spoil the appetite of those around you. After finishing the soup, rest the soup spoon inside the bowl, if it is flat and large, otherwise put it on the saucer under the soup-bowl.

Pastry : Pick up the pastry with the paper napkin when you are served. Put it beside your plate until you are ready to eat. Then either pick up just the pastry, leaving the paper behind, and eat it. If it is served as a dessert course, ease the food out of the paper with your fork and eat it with the same fork.

Mangoes : They should be cut in half-lengthwise. It should be scooped out with a spoon. When eaten at home, they are better enjoyed with your fingers.

Salad: Generally, only the fork is used to eat a salad and to cut lettuce or other greens. But if you meet resistance, using a fork and knife is perfectly correct.

Fruits : A tribute to the calorie-conscious decade is fruits, which are sometimes used as a substitute for dessert. There is no hard-and-fast rule as to how to eat fruits. Since for dinner you will not get peeled or cut fruits, so you can either peel them, cut them and eat with a fork or if you can manage, simply pick up a nice red juicy apple and bite into it — just do whatever is most comfortable for you.

Dessert: It may come with a fork or spoon, depending upon the type of sweet dish.

End of a course: An indication from your side that you are through with the course is by placing your knife and fork side by side in the middle of the plate. If you place them on both sides wide apart that means you are not yet finished.

Toothpicks: Never use them in public.

Tableware

Glasses: The water goblet should rest at the point of your dinner knife. Except for the most formal dinners (where seven courses are served, which is rare these days) a large assortment of glasses is not seen. The use of glassware is easy. For someone will fill the glasses and all you have to do is just drink from it when needed. The water glass is the most obvious and should be kept filled with water. The wine glasses are the long-stemmed delicate ones. If there are two of the same kind, they will be for red and white wine. As you drink from each glass, try to place them back in approximately the same position at the table.

Some other glasses, though not too common, are balloon-shaped brandy glassses, flutes (small-stemmed glasses) for champagne, small glasses for sherry, and port, tumblers for gin, whisky, etc. and large glasses for beer.

Silverware: This has already been discussed and includes: soup spoons, smaller-sized knives and forks for the first course; large-size knives and forks for main course; spoons and forks for the dessert and several other knives and forks which may be supplied to you along with each course. There is a small fork meant for seafood. It will be brought along with the seafood course. It is used for eating shrimps, snails, oysters or any other seafood appetizer. But always remember, it is not to be used for eating fish.

The largest fork is for the main dish — be it meat or fish. And the innermost, slighly smaller fork is for the pudding or dessert. If there is salad, it should be used as salad fork. In such a case, the dessert fork will be brought separately with the course.

The soup spoon is more rounded and hollow than an ordinary spoon and is easily identified.

Dessert spoons or forks may or may not be at the table when you sit down. If they are present, they will either be on the inside positions on both sides of the plate or they will be at the top of the plate. If they are brought with the dessert plate, remove them from the plate and place them beside the plate to facilitate the serving of dessert. Remember, the fork goes on the left and the spoon goes on the right side of the plate.

Knives are always placed with the blades facing towards the plate. Spoons are set with the declivity of their bowl resting on its back. Forks are set with the prongs curving upwards.

Plates : There are two main plates on the table. The bigger main course plate and a side-plate for bread, salad, cheese etc. Soup-bowls and dessert plates will be brought in separately.

Another small extra plate on the dinner plate is often seen in restaurants these days. It is meant to hold the seafood or appetizer or the soup. In fact, it is a superflous plate. Its only function is to protect the dinner plate until it is used. Don't worry unnecessarily about it. The waiter will remove it if it isn't needed. For the main dinner, only the main big dinner plate, which will be quite obvious, should be used.

Napkins: Table napkins can be laid in the centre of a plate or on the side-plate. They can either be folded simply in four or made into complex shapes. But whatever the design, a napkin should always look and feel freshly laundered. Napkins are shaken out as soon as the diner is seated. At a formal dinner, the napkin is picked up only after the host has unfolded his. Unhappily, any sensible method such as securing it in your belt or tucking a corner into your neckline, so it becomes a bib, is not the done thing. On children, a bib-like napkin may be used. Hands are wiped on napkins, lips are dabbed but using it as a face-towel is absolutely out. At the end of the meal, the napkin should be left on the table in a crumpled state. It should not be refolded. Refolding suggests that you have not used it and may mistakenly be given to another person without being laundered.

Enjoy a hearty meal but remember no matter how much you have appreciated it, refrain from smacking your lips or belching loudly.

EATING OUT

There are two reasons why a person eats out:
- *To give oneself a change from the lousy food being provided at home; and*
- *To get a break from the thankless task of preparing such food that goes unappreciated at home.*

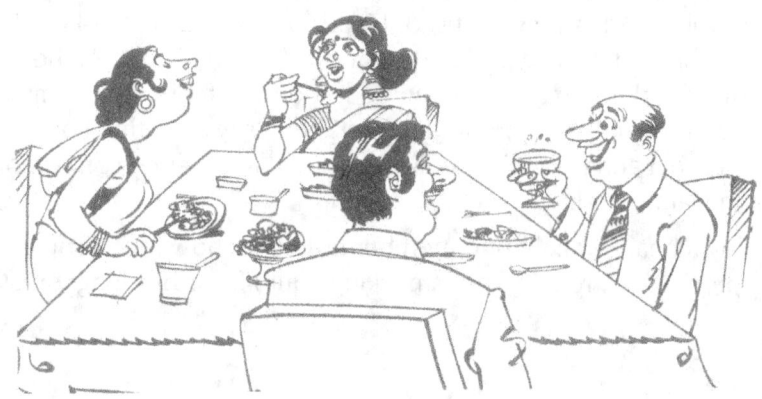

E ating out in a fashionable restaurant can be quite an unnerving experience for a novice. Even old hands are sometimes upstaged by the unexpected. The retinue of waiters and sense of everyone else being totally at ease can easily convince the uninitiated that they are doing the wrong thing and further undermine their self-confidence. A spot of bluffing and bravado may save your day as this is definitely not the place to feel even remotely ill at ease. Sailing through with confidence largely depends upon your knowing what to expect.

Choosing the Place

First of all, choose the place where you want to go for dinner. Consideration should not be given to only the prices but to other things such as the quality and type of food and the variety the restaurant offers.

Decide before leaving whether you want to go to an Indian, Mughlai, South Indian, Chinese, French or Continental restaurant. Also keep in mind the people that frequent a particular restaurant. You can hardly take your family to a nightclub nor can you expect to have a quiet, romantic dinner for two at a noisy fast-food joint.

Booking a Table

Once you have decided upon the place, its always better to book a table in advance to avoid unnecessary waiting at the peak hour there. This will ensure you good and prompt service. Remember to reach the restaurant well in time, to avoid having missed your chance. Restaurants usually give 15-20 minutes grace period before they give your reservation to the person next in queue.

The table should be booked in one person's name — usually the head of the family, for a given number of persons for a specific hour. Due to heavy rush at restaurants, you can double-book a table at two different restaurants just to be sure you won't be without a single reservation. For their own convenience, people book tables at different restaurants and decide at the last minute which one they prefer. This can be very unfair for restaurateurs as they lose out on potential customers if you do not show up. Courtesy demands that you at least cancel the booking at the restaurants which you have dropped.

Arriving

On arrival, the person in whose name the table is booked should check at the reception desk that the booking is in order. Then the headwaiter (*maitre d' hotel*) leads the way to the table, followed by the host and the rest of the party.

Seating

The host can suggest where the guests should sit. If only two persons are at the table, in normal course they would sit across the table opposite each other. A romantically inclined couple may prefer to sit side by side.

If it is a large family group, the head of the family sits at the top of the table with his wife and other important guests sitting next to him on both the sides of the table facing each other. If you are just a foursome, say two couples, then the wives may prefer to sit together and leave the men to talk shop undisturbed.

If children are present, they should be seated close to the parents, preferably the mother, who can restrain them from any unseemly activities as well as keep an eye on their table manners.

Restaurants do not provide high chairs for small kids, so do not even request for one. Bring your own folding chair or leave the baby at home with an elderly person or trusted servant.

Ordering Drinks

As soon as you are seated, the waiter will come and fill up your water glasses and wait for your drinks order. Do not put your guests in a tight spot by adopting a hesitant attitude about drinks and by saying, 'I'm not sure if I want a drink. Do you?'

There is every reason for this statement to make everyone uncomfortable about ordering their drinks as guests usually follow the trend of the host.

Even if you are not planning to order any drinks for yourself, don't say so. Simply ask the others — 'What would you like to have?' This gives a clean chit to your guests who will be able to order drinks with an easy mind, irrespective of whether you drink or not.

The Menu

The menu at a restaurant is likely to be long, detailed and extensive. At many continental restaurants, it may even be written in the vernacular like Chinese or Japanese or French and so on. There usually is an English menu but in its absence or that of an English translation, it is better to ask the waiter about the dishes. Here, 'ignorance is *not* bliss' because you may end up ordering certain unpalatable dishes.

If you come across some new and unusual sounding dishes and wish to try them, it is perfectly okay and the done thing is to ask the waiter how that particular dish is cooked or what it consists of before making up your mind.

Placing the Order

The host or the head of the group (in short, the one who has to pay the bill) does the ordering. Because, as a rule, the waiter places the bill in front of the person who places the orders. It may happen that the waiter approaches your table to take your order before you and your guests are ready to place the order. In this case, the host tells the waiter that they need a little more time to consider. You are not obliged to order as soon as the waiter approaches you. If you are at a business lunch and formality is to be observed, the first order will be placed by the guest of honour.

The host should consider everyone's choice and give everyone a chance to choose a particular dish. An attentive host concerns himself with the ordering and listens to who is choosing what. Once everyone has decided on the dishes, the waiter may be called and the host gives him the entire order. Orders for starters and the main course are placed together so that there is no time gap between the servings. Dessert, however, may be ordered later on after the meal is over. After a particularly filling meal, some people may prefer having coffee to dessert, so leave the option open till after the meal.

Using Spoons, Forks, etc.

The use of spoons, forks, and knives has already been discussed. Restaurants usually do not clutter the table with a profusion of cutlery. A soup spoon will be brought if you have ordered soup. Picking up chicken bones with your fingers is permissible.

Playing Host

A host at a dinner in a restaurant should show the same concern for guests as he would at home. Asking the waiter to fill the glasses, empty the ashtrays, changing an order if a guest is displeased with his food — it's too hot (chilly) or too cold and insisting on sending it back — it is the responsibility of the host to voice such problems on their behalf. When the meal is over, ask the waiter for the check. Years of experience and observation have made waiters astute enough to single out the host in a group of people and will present the check to him. If it's a family, the father gets the check.

As a Guest

As a guest, you are supposed to follow the host's lead. Try to make as little fuss as possible over placing the order, quality of food and the service. It is not the restaurant authorities you will be insulting but indirectly you are blaming your host for bringing you here.

While the host is placing the order, keep quiet. Do not interrupt. Even if he has forgotton something, you can remind him after he has finished giving the order.

In between the meals, if you want to order something extra, tell your host who will ask the waiter for it.

Even while ordering, do not talk about the rates like, 'Let's order this dish, it's cheaper.' or 'Oh, this one is so expensive, let's skip it.' If you are so concerned about the price factor, quietly choose moderately priced dishes.

Take no notice of the check. Do not even try to sneak a look at the bill while the host is making the payment, it looks indecent.

Tipping

Tipping the waiter is very important in a good restaurant, especially if you plan to come back again. Although in some restaurants, the tip is included in the bill itself as service charges, the general practice is that you leave some money apart from the bill as a tip.

Remember, the *maitre d' hotel* (who showed you to your table and took your order) and the busboy (who clears the dishes and pours water) are not to be tipped separately. It is the waiter who is serving you directly who gets the tip, and shares it with them later on. If there is only one waiter, waiting upon you (no *maitre'd' hotel* or busboy), then the tip should be about 5-10 per cent of the amount. Suppose your bill has come to around 200 rupees, the tip you should leave is 20 rupees. If others are present, then the tip should be 15 per cent of the total bill since the amount will be shared by them.

Apart from Eating...

Spotting friends: Suppose you spot a friend on entering the restaurant, just wave and smile unless you have something urgent to say. If you do, have your group seated properly, place the order and then stroll over. But make sure to keep your visit brief, an extra person standing in between tables tends to cause confusion. Besides, the group in which the person you are talking to may want to resume their original conversation. If friends drop by at your table, introduce them to everyone, leaving out the formality of shaking hands.

Calling the waiter: Whereas it can be exasperating not to be able to attract the attention of a waiter, dramatic or brash gestures should be avoided. If he seems to be deliberately avoiding your table, the best approach would be to speak to the manager, explaining that you have been waiting quite a while for service. He may put another waiter to wait upon your table.

In the usual course, wait until your waiter passes your table to claim his attention. Never interrupt his waiting upon another table.

Table Manners for Children

Children being children are neither intimidated by the splendour of a restaurant nor can they be stopped from satisfying their natural curiosities. They would like to roam about, touching everything and getting the feel of the place. To stop them from coming in people's ways and generally making a nuisance of themselves, the best way is to try to keep their attention diverted. Engage them in some verbal word game or conversation. By wandering around the place, they may come in the way of the waiters and cause accidents. Above all, they should not play hide-and-seek under the tables. This has led to many disasters involving crockery being broken and an irate manager is justified in asking you to reimburse the damage. Any shouting at the waiter or talking loudly should be curbed immediately. The elders should serve them and supervise their eating. Making noises while eating, slurping while drinking, spilling or throwing food during the meal, improper use of spoon and fork are some noticeably bad table manners which, unfort-unately, are noticed in kids only at a restaurant.

Table Manners

Sitting down: Always sit down from the right side of the chair. This is especially important for women who are being seated by a waiter. For this is what the waiter will expect you to do when he pulls the chair out for you. Without being stiff, make an effort to sit up straight at the table. It is now permissible to put an elbow on the table between courses or when you are talking after dinner. Just be careful not to rely on your elbows alone for support — you may end up with your nose in the soup. Do not dig your elbows into the sides of both your neighbours.

Using a napkin: A napkin is not just to be used on your lap. Use it to remove food crumbs from your lips. Dab at your lips between mouthfuls to avoid any crumbs being left behind and also before using a glass as this prevents a messy rimmed glass.

Making conversation: No one likes a loudmouth, specially a person who speaks with his mouth full. Avoid dominating a table conversation dinner and speak only on pleasant topics. Details of illness, surgery, funerals, reptiles and anything that could make someone squeamish are the topics to be avoided. Avoid a topic that is likely to be the centre of a heated debate.

Reaching across the table: Earlier, reaching across the table used to be strictly taboo. Reaching across the table not only looks ungainly but can also cause accidents like spilling water or knocking a plate over the edge. Avoid stretching in front of another person to reach a particular dish. All you have to do is to ask for it to be passed to you.

Pests in the food: Occasionally, a water glass or a curry may arrive with a small insect in it. The correct way to handle this is it not to draw the attention of the others to it, but quietly request the waiter to remove the offending dish or glass and bring you a fresh one. The same technique should be used for unclean silverware or dishes. Don't raise a ruckus.

Removing food from your mouth: If you wish to remove a piece of food from your mouth, never spit it out noisily or use your fingers to extract it. Bring the spoon you are using close to your mouth and spit out whatever it is you want noiselessly. Seeds, pits and small bones obviously cannot be swallowed. So remove them by cupping your hand over your mouth and place them on the side of your plate.

Eating food that is too hot: If you take a bite of food that is too hot to swallow, push it down with water as discreetly as possible. Never spit it out.

Ketchup, jams, jellies and butter: Pour ketchup, mustard or any other bottled sauce directly on the food you want to eat it with. If it is French fries, do not drench them in the sauce. Rather pour a small amount of ketchup on the side of the plate and dip the French fries in it as you eat them.

Jams and jellies are transferred to the serving plate with a spoon and then spread on the bread with the butter knife.

Small pieces of butter are picked up with a fork. Then the same butter knife can be used to spread it.

Never use a piece of bread to wipe your plate clean.

Dropped items: Anyone can drop a spoon or fork or food. So don't be ashamed if you do so. Just ask the waiter to replace whatever it is you have dropped. Don't attempt to search for the dropped item by scrambling on all fours. Forget about it for the time being. At the conclusion of the meal, you can quietly reach for whatever is dropped. Or leave it for the waiters when they clean up the place. Similarly, if some food has been dropped on the table, just leave it alone. Later, if you can remove the small particles of food discreetly to your plate with a napkin, do so, otherwise leave it.

Once you've finished: Do not push your plate away from you after you have finished your meal. A general rule of thumb is to serve the dishes from the left and remove from the right. When you are through eating, place your cutlery side by side in the centre of your plate and leave your napkin in its crumpled state by your plate.

To smoke or not to: It is never polite to smoke during a meal. It is only civilized to refrain from smoking while anyone at the table is still eating or anyone indicates that he is allergic to the smoke or if you notice that someone appears to be annoyed by the smoke. After the meal, when coffee is served, you can light up a cigarette after taking permission from the others.

Using finger bowls: In instances where you may have eaten with your hands, finger bowls are brought to you after the meal to clean your fingers without having to get up from the table. They are brought with fine lemon slices. If the dessert is not served with the *thali* itself, then the finger bowl is used before it is brought to the table. The technique of using a finger bowl is very simple. Dip your fingers into the water. Rub on the slice of lemon and dry your hands on the napkin. Then leave the napkin unfolded on the table as refolding suggests that the napkin was not used at all and it can be given to another person.

End of the meal : An indication that you are through with the meal is by placing your knife and fork or spoon and the fork side by side in the middle of the plate. If you place them wide apart on each side of the plate, that means you are not yet finished.

Thank You's

A restaurant meal is always thanked for on the spot. A telephone call of thanks may be repeated the next day, but a thanks immediately after dinner is a must. A thank-you note is also appreciated.

PARTY TIME

'Rules never made a good party:

Imagination, spontaneity and a commitment to doing things well is far nearer the mark.'

The Occasion

Generally speaking, any date is good for a party. It needs no other excuse than itself. That reminds me of a friend of mine who once threw a big bash. On asking what the occasion was, he flashed a smile and replied, 'Because it's Friday.' — as simple as that. But unfortuantely most of us find ourselves so preoccupied with our work that it is only on some special occasion that we celebrate and throw parties like on a birthday, anniversary, engagement party or at times, a promotion celebration. But try giving a surprise party sometime — it will change the mood of life.

Although there is no fixed 'code of conduct' for throwing a party still there are certain rigid principles that are applied at any party. One of them is that the degree of success of the occasion is determined by the guest list.

Choosing the Guests

Priority should be given to planning an appropriate mix of guests — just like you would mix a cocktail. You have to consider the impact of guests on the others. It is a good practice to combine some familiar faces with new ones. The main criterion is to consider whether people will actually like, mingle and stimulate each other. Choosing guests with common interests is a good idea.

Another area to watch out for is that guests do not turn the party over to shop talk which may exclude other fellow guests. Try and include all your guests in the conversation. If it is a very large party, groups will form and you cannot control the thread of conversation in every group.

Three talkers to five listeners is a good formula when making your guest list. If you invite only non-stop talkers, you will end up with a cacophany and no one listening. On the other hand, a gathering of the strong silent types and introverts may produce a boring evening with each uncommunicative guest waiting for someone else to take the lead.

Compiling a guest list for a big party is simpler when compared to a small intimate gathering, because a mix which might be uncomfortable in that small intimate gathering is not likely to pose any problem in a crowd.

Invitations

Guests are issued verbal invitations well in advance. These may be telephoned or extended in person. Even when you are sending written notes or invitation cards, it is still expected of you to ring up and invite the guests personally. If you do not have a telephone facility or your guests are fussy about personal invitations – in both the cases, it's better to go to their house and invite them personally and hand over the card at the same time.

Pressing the Guests for Acceptance

Although guests should not be forced to come, it is common practice to press them twice or thrice before accepting their inability to attend the function. The conversation may run something like this:

You: "The function is on Friday. All of you must come."

Guest: "Well, I'm not sure, my cousin will be here around that time."

You: "So what? Bring your cousin along as well. It would be fun."

Guest: "O.K. I'll try my best to attend."

Accepting and Declining Invitations

There is no fixed format for accepting or declining an invitation in India. 'I'll try my best' is the usual phrase. In fact, we Indians, prefer to leave much to chance rather than confirm it. A total decline of an invitation can only be in the event of going out of town, an illness or death in the family, etc.

If you accept an invitation, be sure to go to the party, unless the above-mentioned circumstances prevent you from doing so at the last minute. If this happens, please ring your host and apologize for the inconvenience caused.

Planning a Menu

Guests are always delighted by good food, so to make your party successful, a careful planning of the menu is essential. Whatever be the nature of the gathering, homely or formal, the menu is important.

It is impolite to serve a hastily put together slapdash meal which would give the guests the impression that they were scarcely worth bothering about. Do not choose dishes that require you to be in the kitchen for the better part of the evening. Guests will not only feel neglected but also guilty about not being able to offer any help. If you have servants to do the cooking and serving, you may not have this problem. Otherwise rely upon advance preparation and the minimum of culinary attention during the party. Only last-minute details should be left.

Keen cooks usually seize this opportunity to try out a new dish. The best advice would be to serve only those dishes that you are confident of doing a superb job of. With untried recipes, there are chances of its turning into a fiasco. Cooking fiascos may be overlooked in an intimate gathering but at a large party, you may well end up being the joke of the evening.

Menu

A general menu for a party should include a variety of items, so that everyone gets a chance to eat something or the other of his choice.

For example, at a birthday party, at the beginning serve drinks and light snacks consisting of chips, wafers or if you prefer, *pakoras*, cutlets or *samosas*. Then comes the cake-cutting ceremony, candles are blown out and the cake is cut and everybody sings for the birthday boy or girl and gets a piece of cake.

Now comes the main dinner. The vegetarian menu can include one *dal*, or *rajma* or *chhole* with two dry vegetables and one or two gravy dishes like butter *paneer/dum alu/ malai kofta* and *raita*, *papad*, pickle, *salad,* etc. should be there. If you can arrange *romali roti/tandoori roti/nan,* etc. from a nearby restaurant, nothing like it. Then all you will have to do in the kitchen, at the last moment, is to make the vegetable *pulao*. However, if you have a cook, hot *chapatis/paranthas/pooris* can be served. But do not plan them if you have to make them yourself because you cannot afford to be tied up in the kitchen and neglect your guests. As for your nonvegetarian guests, serve them hot *kebabs* and *tikkas* as snacks with drinks. For dinner, replace one gravy dish with *keema kofta* or butter chicken and one dry one with a dry nonveg. dish like *keema mutter* etc.

Nonvegetarian food tastes better with dry bread so do not make *poori* or *parantha* with it. The *pulao* can be replaced with *biryani*. But remember that a nonvegetarian dinner should be a combination of both vegetarian and nonvegetarian dishes. Many people enjoy nonveg. dishes as a change, but what ultimately satisfies their palate is vegetarian food.

Your Role

As host/hostess, you must be there to welcome each guest individually, perform introductions, seat everyone, urge the guests to feel at home, ply them with drinks and snacks, indicate where the

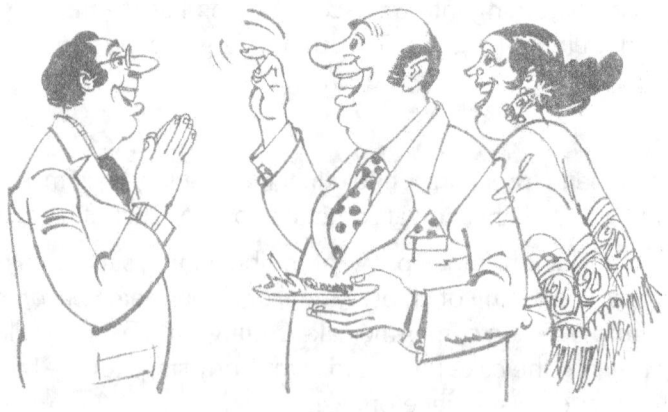

washroom and toilet are, circulate freely among them so no one feels left out, have an appropriate selection of music ready to play, etc.

Food Taboos

When inviting people, be sure you know of their eating habits and the type of food they may or not eat. Around the table at a dinner party, may be seated Brahmins (no meat, fish, not even onion and garlic), slightly less orthodox Punjabis (no meat on Tuesdays), vegetarians (no meat at all), Jains (a very very limited variety of foods) and vegans (no dairy produce or meat or fish) and last, but not the least, those on a diet.

If you are a nonvegetarian and you invite people whom you very well know are strict vegetarians, it would be discourteous to offer them a meal consisting largely of meat. Furthermore, if your invitees are a combination of both vegetarian and nonvegetarians, both types of dishes should be there. In fact, there can be more of vegetarian dishes than that of nonvegetarian because the vegetarian can only eat vegetarion, whereas the nonvegetarian guests can relish and enjoy both kinds of dishes.

If it is an intimate, small gathering and you are in doubt as to how best to cater to your friends' special tastes and requirements, the best counsel can come from them.

Party Prescriptions

The secret of a successful party is elusive. Till date, no one has come upon a fool-proof method. In one way, this is good or else all parties would be on the same lines and hence, be boring.

Choosing guests who have common interests and enjoy each other's company is one guideline for a successful party.

Never be a miser about hospitality. Because of uncertainties of appetite, more food will have to be produced than is actually consumed. Some waste is almost unavoidable.

Keep a well-stocked bar. It will never do for you to run short of drinks just when the party has picked up momentum. This is guaranteed to dampen even the most enthusiastic of spirits. No matter how much liquor a person consumes, they should not get the feeling that you are counting every glass that they drink.

Arriving at a Party

Timing your arrival at a party is very tricky business. Unpunctuality has become fashionable and it is a common practice to reach a party not less than half an hour late.

Believe me, if you are on time, you may find your hostess still in her curlers and the room still in the process of being cleaned. And the expression on your host's face will be more than enough to make you realize your folly. So if a party is scheduled for 7:30 p.m., never reach before 8.30 p.m., unless the host stresses punctuality.

Uninvited Guests

There are times when you are all set to go to a party and an unexpected guest turns up at your house. There are only two options open to you – either take him with you or you stay back, cancelling the dinner appointment. If your guest is familiar with the people who are throwing the party, you may take him along. But in both the cases, whether you are going or not, it is your duty to call up the host and inform him about the unexpected situation. Take your guest to the party with you only after getting permission from the host. It is discourteous to take him along to the party without informing your host beforehand.

As a host/hostess, welcome even the uninvited guests. You cannot go into a sulk for the rest of the evening just because Mr X has brought Mr A or Mr B with him.

Return Gifts

It is your birthday and you've been planning a celebration days in advance. If you have made it known to your invitees that it's your birthday, you can be sure of being at the receiving end of many gifts. Wait a minute! Your son attended a child's birthday party last week and not only did he give the birthday boy a gift but received one in return too. You break out in cold sweat. You don't have return gifts for your guests. Relax – this custom is prevalent among children's parties. It does not apply to adults. You are throwing a party with good food and wine, good music — what more can you give. Definitely not a return gift to each of your guests.

Goodbyes and Thank-you's

Remember to take your leave at a reasonable hour. A host may take it personally as a signal indicating the failure of his party if people start leaving the party early. And it is a tendency that if one couple leaves, others won't be too far behind. So early leave-takers should bear this in mind. It is therefore probably wisest for a guest aiming at an early get-away to make a quiet exit without saying goodbye formally to everyone, leaving the host to explain his absence. It can wreck the mood of the party. Unquestionably, it is courteous to ring up the next day and say thank you. What a host most wishes to hear is that you had a good time. So be generous in your compliments concerning the food, drink or table decorations.

Parties for All Occasions

Birthday/anniversary: It is is usually a dinner party and the guest list consists mainly of your relatives and close friends.

People start coming around between 7:30 and 8 p.m. The drinks and snacks are served. The cake is cut and after some time, the dinner is announced. Gifts from the guests to the host/hostess are a compulsory part of the celebrations.

Promotion: It is generally given inviting office colleagues and some close friends. If you want to share the occasion with your relatives as well, it's better to give them a separate party if you can afford it. Also since your elders would be present, it may constrain you and your friends and colleagues from really enjoying yourselves. Rest of the proceedings are much the same except for cutting the cake.

Chat party: At a chat party instead of the usual dinner you arrange for *chat.* You can hire a *chatwala* to do the *chat* making for you. If you have invited a handful of friends its not difficult to make it yourself. Drinks are also served.

Chat parties are usually scheduled from 6 p.m. to 8 p.m. They can even start at 7 p.m. and go up to as late as 10 p.m.

On a larger scale, a proper catering party is engaged. They set up various stalls in an open space — your lawn or terrace. Each stall serves different items like *tikki, papri, golgappas,* fruit *chat* and so on. You go to the desired stall and take your pick. Waiters and servants do not serve here, except for the drinks. It is a self-service system.

Bar-be-cue: Bar-be-cues are for those who relish roasted non-greasy stuff. Since it's an open air party, it is best held when the weather is just changing — early spring or late autumn. Readymade bar-be-cues are available in the market and are easy to set up. It grills and roasts the food without any application of oil. It is basically like an oven (*angeethi*) and charcoal is used in it for cooking. *Kebabs, tikkas,* fish *tikkas, paneer tikkas, tandoori* chicken, roasted potatoes, cauliflour, etc. can be deliciously turned out on a bar-be-cue. Guests may stand or sit around. Napkins may be given with plates, but no spoons or forks are necessary.

Kitty parties : Kitty parties have become the in-thing among ladies of all classes and social status. Ladies get together in their free time and play cards or other games such as *tambola*. All ladies belonging to one kitty contribute a certain fixed amount of money every month to it. The lady in whose house the kitty party for the month is going to be held, arranges for the snacks or lunch (whatever is the rule in their kitty). When the ladies get together at her house, soft drinks and snacks are first served. Then some games are played like *Tambola, Rummy* or *Paploo*. Another round of drinks is followed by some gossip (an essential ingredient for a ladies' party) and the collection of money. The lady of the house is entitled to this collected money. Each member gets to throw one party a year and this is how the money is evenly distributed.

A kitty party is never a dinner party, it is only held during the day because that is the time the ladies are free. It can either be a lunch or a high-tea party. After lunch, another round of coffee, mingled with gossip, follows.

Children at a party
Children are generally adorable. But at a party, specially when the naughty ones find their parents busy, they can be quite a nuisance. However, if you stop taking them to parties or do not let them help you in organizing one at home just because you find they get in the way, it is likely to hamper their growth in later years. Children who

have helped you in preparing for a party and have shared family meals at which visitors were present or attended parties with you are more likely to be able to manage their own social life in later years in a much better way than those who have been neglected in this area.

Small babies at parties

Taking a small baby with you to a party means his feeds and nappies have to be attended to. If you have reliable servants or elders, leave very small children at home. If you have an *ayah*, take her along too to a party so she can look after the baby. Else use disposable diapers for the baby. They are readily available in the market and the baby does not feel wet or uncomfortable either, for at least three-four hours. Bottle-fed babies can be fed in public, but for breast-feeding, your hostess can provide you with a secluded room.

Young visitors

Even though it is the parents' responsibility to ensure a child's good behaviour and prevent them from becoming nuisances, it is advisable that the hostess allot a separate room to the kids with various games, toys, video games or a suitable movie to keep them occupied. The snacks, drinks and even the dinner can be served to them there itself. This is a sure method to keep both the parties happy.

Solving a dispute

If there is a minor dispute among the children, do not give it too much importance and solve it with your quick reasoning. But if you find it getting out of hand, try some disciplinary tactics. If this does not work either, then inform their respective parents before handing out any strict punishments.

If you know by experience that the kids invited to the party are naughty, it will be a good idea to keep all breakable and expensive things out of their reach. This will prevent any damage from taking place, you losing your temper and the parents of the kids are spared any kind of embarrassment on their children's behalf.

A CHILDREN'S PARTY

'You'll need a bloody big house
With a football field for a table
For your cute little guests.
For a run-of-the-mill formal
With these thirty-five little guests
You'll need, at least three for every five,
twenty-one servants.'

Children's parties require three essentials — a non-stop programme of entertainment, a surprising amount of stamina and an unlimited exuberance. At a birthday party I had attended last year, a roomful of little ones were busy bursting crackers and balloons, and hurling streamers, when this little fellow sidled up to me and asked politely: "Please, when is the party going to begin?"

Children's parties almost revolve around the bringing of presents for the young party-giver. Guests arrive with their offerings in hand. And the child that comes empty handed had better be warned

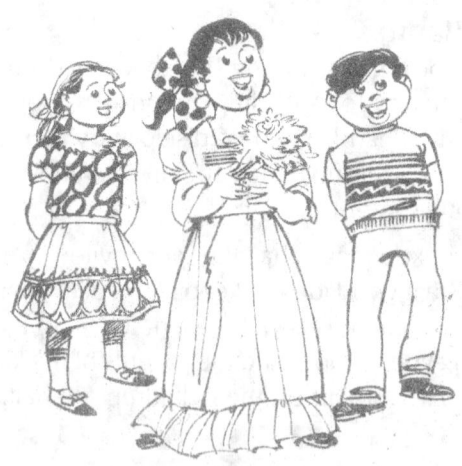

that not only has he made an enemy of the kid whose birthday it is but it is, highly unlikely that others present will invite him to any of their future parties. The party generally ends with the invitees departing satisfied with a small return present and having gorged themselves silly.

Party Occasions

Children's parties are usually birthday celebrations. But with more westernized culture catching on in our society, Christmas (25th December) and Halloween (31st October) also offer a good excuse to throw a children's party.

The Guest List

School-children, in particular, have strong likes and dislikes among their age group. This, at times, gives rise to the issue of who can be omitted from the guest-list. It is not good manners as the gesture is hurtful to the child left out and in future may prove to be the cause of a withdrawn, cold person. Parents should be firm on this matter and if you are inviting the whole class, no one should be left out as a general principle. Also, the guest list should include those who have invited the young host to their own parties. Don't forget to invite children from neighbouring houses or apartments. The age-group should also be kept in mind. Everyone should be more or less in the same age bracket. Don't invite teenagers to an under-10 party. Except, of course, if you are throwing a huge party with a range of diversions suitable for different age-groups.

Among adults who may appreciate an invitation are the grandparents, some close family friends and other fond relatives. It is also a courteous thought to invite the host child's teacher to the party.

Invitations

Special invitations for children's parties are available in the market. They strike a party note with a perky drawing on the cover. As a rule, they also have handy tear-off replies which can be sent by the invitees individually, well in advance, so as to enable the host to make the preparations accordingly.

The card should give the time at which the party begins and ends, the full address where the occasion is to be held, an address and telephone number for RSVP, and the reason for the party, e.g. 'Rita's birthday'. In case two children of the same family are being invited, it is thoughtful to send each a separate card as receiving the invitation is part of the fun.

Timing

Punctuality is the rule as festivities begin on the dot. Parties for young children, in general, start at around 5-6 p.m. and end promptly by 7.30 or 8.00 p.m. Teenagers tend to prefer to imitate a grown-up style in which case, the timing is determined by the activities. However, the hours should still be specified on the invitation.

Games

A children's party can never be complete without some games or other forms of entertainment.

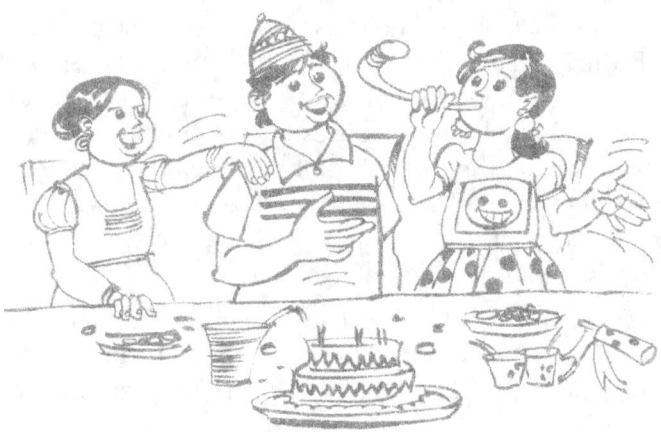

Very small children, below three-four years, can be given toys to play with like stuffed animals, etc. and left to themselves until it is time for cutting the cake.

Older children, however, can, choose from a wider variety of games. If you have a huge lawn and space is available for outside games, children will love it and seeing their enthusiasm, you too will be infused with the spirit of the party. Apart from the usual races and other games, you can have one or more of the following games.

Dodge ball: The children are divided into two groups. Two concentric circles are formed and the team on the outer circle is given the ball. Their aim is to hit the inner team, who try and dodge the ball within the confines of the circle, on their legs. All those hit by the ball are declared out and those who are able to dodge the ball remain in the game. The last person is declared the winner.

Eagle and the mother bird: All children except one stand behind one another holding onto the person in front by the waist. The first in the line is the strong mother-bird and those behind him are the young ones. The singled out person is the eagle. The eagle tries to catch the young one while the mother bird tries to save them. All those caught by the eagle fall out of the line.

Finding the partner: Two groups are made. Children in one group are paired off with those in the second group. Then they are all made to run haphazardly as music is played. As soon as the music stops, they immediately set about finding their respective partners and on doing so, quickly sit down. All those standing who have not been able to find their partners are out.

Musical chairs: This is a very common and popular game played at children's parties. Chairs — one less than the total number of children playing the game — are set up in the centre of the room. Music is played and the children are asked to run around the chairs. As soon as the music stops, the children are to find seats for themselves. Since there is one less chair, the child left standing will be out. Now one more chair is removed and the game is repeated, and soon till the last chair is left.

If there is not enough space available for outdoor activities, there are various indoor games that can be good entertainment for your little guests.

Housy or lotto: It is a fun-game similar to Tambola and is very common among older children these days. It can be bought from the market and played as per the instructions.

Passing the parcel: A big parcel containing lots of sweets and other goodies is made. A number of chits in accordance with the number of children playing are made separately containing various instructions like sing, dance, leap like a frog, make ten faces, laugh for five minutes, etc. The parcel is passed around the children who sit in a circle and music is played. The music is stopped every few minutes and whichever child is holding the parcel when the music is stopped, takes a chit out of the bowl and has to act according to the instructions. After performing his act, he is asked to step out of the circle. The last person of the group gets the parcel as his present.

Rewards

One most important thing to remember is that for each game, separate presents should be given out. There is no need to distribute expensive gifts — pencils, rubbers or chocolates or some hankies can be distributed as presents. Make sure each child gets something even if just a toffee so as not to feel left out.

Refreshments

By the time the games are over, the whole group would be ravenous. Bring them to the table where the cake is to be cut. After cutting the cake, refreshments should be served. Heavy, greasy stuff is not for children. *Poori, kachauri, bhaturas* are not liked by the children. They need something light. But there should be variety. Just keep in mind how fussy your own child is in his eating habits. The best choice may be two-three types of sandwiches, biscuits, chips, noodles (all the kids love them these days — thanks to the Maggi noodles ad.), and if you wish, grilled cheese *tikkas*. And of course, cake and soft drinks. Don't force the children to eat more than they can. Just keep a watchful eye on the proceedings. Believe me, they will eat much better if left to their own devices.

Goodbyes

As already said, a return present is a must for a children's party. Prepare them in advance before the party, and just hand one to each child as they bid you and the little host goodbye.

TRAVEL TIME

Two men were seated next to each other in an aeroplane. Somehow they couldn't get an interesting conversation going however much they tried. Worse still, they kept getting into an argument every time a topic was broached. A third passenger seated alongside them got so fed up that after witnessing the third verbal spat, he snarled at the two and ordered them to go outside and come back only after settling the issue. They did exactly that.

And they were back in time for the plane to take off.

*T*ravelling is a time for enjoyment, fun and frolic. A breather, a change of environment, renewed energy to cope with future problems is what travelling provides us. But it may prove one hell of a time, if you venture out without doing proper homework. So whenever you are travelling, just do some preplanning, make appropriate arrangements and you will certainly love the outing.

Planning

To derive the maximum benefit out of your trip, try to get as much information as you possibly can about the place you intend visiting. Talk to friends and acquaintances who have been there before. Tips like places to stay and visit, good eating places, the weather conditions and what clothes to take are going to be very useful.

Always remember, half the fun of travelling lies in its preparation and planning. Comfortable clothes, shoes, proper food and a nice place to stay make a lot of difference.

Choosing a Place

Before you start planning the food, shelter, itinerary, etc., make sure your primary condition is fulfilled, i.e. the choice of the place.

Don't go about your travel schedule in the manner where you first pack everything, make arrangements back home, then sit down to think of an appropriate place to go. The first thing should be the choice of a fixed destination. Once decided, you may try to glean more information about the place, then prepare accordingly. If it is summer, chose a place with a cool climate, or a hillstation. If it is winter, go to the seaside.

Foreign Travel

If you have decided to go on a foreign trip, application for a pas port and visa must be made at least four to six weeks in advance. If these have already been obtained, then their validity should be checked.

Mode of Transport

The mode of transport should be chosen keeping two things in mind — first, of course, is your budget and secondly, the comfort. If you can afford it and the place is air-linked, nothing like it. It's easier, simpler and the fastest mode of transport.

In case you are going by train or bus, then reservations must be done in advance. Scenic beauty and a close rapport with various people is something you can only get during a train or bus journey.

If you have small children, it is always desirable to travel either by air or by train. Bus journeys should be avoided as various facilities like toilet, easy movement, more space, sleeping berths, water taps, are not readily available.

Reservations

Once decided upon the mode of transport, bookings should be made as soon as possible, in fact, immediately (before you change your mind or all seats are reserved) so that you have confirmed seats. These can either be done directly at the Railway Station or Bus Stand or Airline Office, or through a travel agency.

Travel Agency

Don't get involved with a travel agency unless you are absolutely sure about its credentials. By availing yourself of the services of a travel agency, this problem of confirming tickets no longer rests with you. Since travel is their business, the agency can execute jobs faster and far more economically than individuals.

Valuable services like hotel stays, transportation, sightseeing trips, etc. are provided by the agency at no extra cost, since they get a commission from various airlines, hotels, etc. They are also well-versed with details such as group tours, concessions at various places, charters and off-season rates for hotels. The best way to approach a travel agency is by going through a person familiar with one. Explain your budget, intended destination, mode of travel and date, including the duration of the trip and the number of persons travelling. In fact, the more the details, the better.

Now, just sit back and relax till your travel agency calls you to collect your tickets. In case of a foreign trip, the travel agent can even help you with your passport, and visa, and arrange them in no time.

Preparations at Home

Once these preparations are underfoot, it is the time to begin preparations at home.

Taking leave: All those who have to take permission from their respective schools, colleges or offices, should do so well in advance so that you are not refused leave at the last minute.

List of things: It is always better to make out a list of things you might require during the journey, for example the kind of clothes, depending upon the weather there. Limit their number to the barest minimum. It is always good to travel light.

Packing: It is better to carry small suitcases. It is neither feasible nor advisable to carry huge, bulging suitcases which no one person will be able to carry by himself, besides it will crumple all your clothes.

One suitcase may be shared by two members of the family or each should carry a bag suitable for easy carrying.

Clothes should be layered, so that they cushion each other. While packing, heavy items should go at the bottom, shoes at the sides, under-garments and kerchiefs in the crannies. Nightgowns and pyjamas go above everything else. Make a list of items and double-check those that are packed to avoid double packing. A classic tip on packing: lay out everything you think you need and leave half of it at home.

Handbag: Apart from the suitcases, you will require hand baggage to hold snacks, a medicine kit, items like soap, comb, paste, etc. to freshen you up during the journey. A thermos flask may be carried separately, if you are going in a big group, otherwise a water bottle which can easily be accommodated inside a bag, is sufficient for a small family.

Entertainment: If you want some entertainment on the journey, it is better to carry a book rather than taking a two-in-one or a transistor which is not only bulky but must be handled with care. Carry a pack of cards or folding games like ludo, snakes and ladders, etc.

Jewellery and money: Make sure you do not carry any jewellery with you. It would be most desirable to wear simple, imitation jewellery and abandon your ornaments for a few days. Keep all your jewellery in a bank locker while you are away.

Even the money you carry, should be either in the form of travellers cheques or if you still insist on carrying cash keep it in two-three separate places. Never keep all your money together at one place or on one person.

Your house

An empty house is an open invitation to the burglars. So, when the entire household leaves on a vacation, some precautions should be observed.

* Leave at least one light on, inside the house.

* Jewelry and other valuables should be put in the bank locker.

* Tell the newspaper hawker and milkman to stop the delivery during these days, so that your front door is not clogged with stacks of newspaper and milk bottles and make it obvious to burglars that no one is at home.

* Tell the *dhobi*, maid-servant, etc. not to come for a few days.

* Switch off and double-check your gas cylinder, iron, TV, geysers, water pump, airconditioner, cooler, and finally, all the locks

before leaving. In case you are going on a long trip, it is better to defrost the fridge and switch it off.

* Inform a trustworthy neighbour or relative about your programme and request him to keep an eye on the house.

* Have your house and its contents insured.

Departure

It is better to take a public transport to the station/airport, if you are going on a long trip. Leave your own vehicle at home safely behind garage doors. However, if it is only for a day or two, you can take your own vehicle and park it at the station/airport/bus-stand in the pay-parking area. They charge very nominal rates and ensure that your vehicle is kept in good condition.

Air Travel

After arriving at the airport, the baggage is taken to the airline counter. The officer on duty examines your tickets. There may be a long queue at the counter, but be patient, it won't take long. And in any case, creating a scene here won't be of much help.

After your tickets have been checked, the baggage is weighed. Standard baggage permitted is 20 kg per passenger travelling on economy class and 30 kg for those travelling in the first class on both domestic and international flights. Baggage that is not required for the duration of travel is checked in, that means it is kept in the storage compartment of the aircraft and delivered on arrival at the destination. Usually, the airlines provides stickers and baggage tags for fixing onto the baggage.

Avoid carrying excess baggage and save yourself the trouble of looking for fellow-passengers to dump some of your excess baggage onto.

After checking the ticket and baggage, the counterfoil is returned by the airline representative with a boarding pass. In case of an international flight, there is a customs, immigration and security check before one actually proceeds towards the aircraft. Nowadays, in order to protect passengers and the aircrafts from hijackers and terrorists, strict security measures have been enforced. Baggage, briefcases and handbags are passed through an X-ray machine and passengers are frisked in small booths by a security officer of the same sex.

Since there is a lot of checking to be done, as a rule, you should reach the airport at least one hour before the domestic flight and three hours prior to an international flight.

Once inside the aircraft, the airhostess will show you your seat. In fact, before going through security, you can indicate to the duty officer your choice of seat regarding the 'Smoking' or 'No smoking' zone or a window or aisle seat.

If you are an economy class passenger and arrive late, your chances of getting a middle seat (the least desirable) are more. This, however, can prove to be quite a bother, specially if the elbows and shoulders of your copassengers keep digging into you.

Train Travel

Travelling by train can be simply delightful or boring, depending upon the kind of trip you are undertaking and your copassengers. If you are on a pleasure trip, there is nothing like train travel — the beautiful scenery outside is bound to put you in a holiday mood immediately. But if it's a business trip, the lengthy journey can prove to be quite boring. The best way to lighten up is by looking

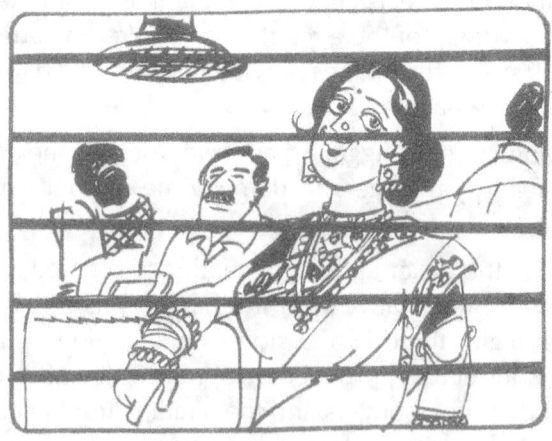

around, befriending your neighbours and inculcating a joyous mood, free from all tensions. Or if you prefer, read a book or magazine on the journey.

Since there is no checking on trains, you can reach the station even at the last minute. But to be on the safe side, it is better to reach there at least half an hour before the scheduled time. Because you will have to first find the platform, then the coach and finally your berth.

Once seated, don't assume the whole coupe is yours. There are others also occupying the same coupe, so keep your belongings in one corner instead of scattering them all over the place.

Train travel brings a cross-section of people together for a long period of time. So it is necessary to be considerate to others.

Bus

For short distances, buses are more comfortable, but they should be avoided on long distances as they prove to be very tedious and tiresome.

Travelling in a bus is much the same as in a train, with the nonavailability of certain amenities. The only consolation being that it is faster and takes you quickly to your destination. If you've got your tickets booked through a travel agent, he may get you on a video coach, in which case you may be able to pass time comfortably watching movies.

There is one person I know of, who once travelled by one of these video coaches from Delhi to Meerut. They were showing a new movie that day. He liked the movie and was watching it very intensely. His disappointment knew no end, when the bus reached Meerut in two hours, with the movie still unfinished. Our good man, not wanting to leave the movie half-finished, went along with the bus till Khatauli where finally the movie got over. There he got down, caught another bus back to Meerut and reached home almost two-and-a-half hours late.

HOUSEGUESTS/VISITORS

'You're stuck.
The expense is yours.
The house is yours.
The guests are yours.
Your only hope is elopement.'

*H*aving people to stay with you is a delicate business. It could be anyone but the enjoyment of their stay partly depends upon you. Friends do not really know each other until they spend a day or two under the same roof. Visits to close relatives or friends rarely pose any problems of either behaviour or dress since you already know them very well but first visits to those who are not particularly close friends, or those who entertain formally can be slightly intimidating.

Duration of a Visit
The length of a visit is for the guest to determine. The distance that they have to travel is the foremost thing in determining the length of their visits. A long and tiring journey will determine the frequency of a person's visits, so when people from far visit, the duration of the visit can be slightly longer. The visitor must remember that he/she is welcome but for a limited period of time.

Arrival
As a rule, house guests are expected to make their own way to the host's place. You are expected to pick them up from the station/airport/bus-stand if they: (a) are elderly people; (b) are new to the place; (c) are arriving at night or very early in the morning; or (d) have extended the same courtesy to you at some point. Dropping them off is positively your duty.

The Welcome
The custom of receiving your guests at the door is as old as hospital-

ity itself. There is no greeting more welcome than finding your host waiting at the door. You should help the guests with their luggage yourself or have your servant do it and show them to their room (if you have a spare guestroom), otherwise wherever you plan to put him/her/them up. The location of toilet and bathroom should be indicated promptly and immediate refreshment offered. Once freshened up and relaxed, you can now sit down for a hearty chat. Yes, it is necessary to make your houseguest feel at home.

Guestroom

If you have a separate guestroom with an attached bath, nothing like it, otherwise you can put your guests in the children's room. If there are only one or two guests, they can share the room with the kids, but if they are more, you can shift out the kids to your own room or to the drawing room. Do not expect your guests to stay in the drawing room, specially if they have come to spend a few days with you. Do so yourself.

All this should be arranged prior to the guests' arrival. Do not hold a family counsel regarding the sleeping arrangements, who is to go where, where the suitcases are to be kept, after your guests have arrived. These should be determined beforehand. The bed should be made with fresh linens. The bathroom should have every neces-sity like soap, toothpaste, shampoo, clean towel, etc. A waste-paper

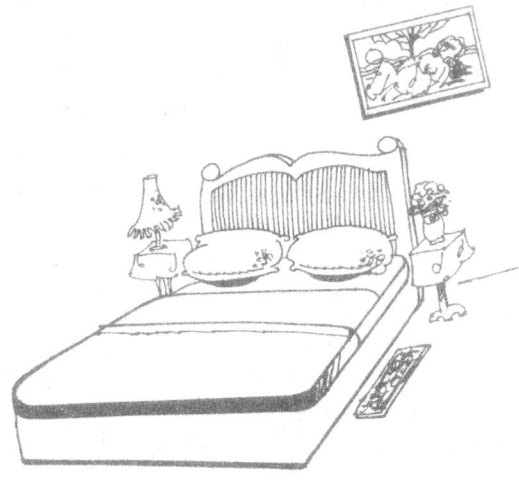

basket should be there in the room. Lighting arrangements should also be appropriate for dressing, grooming and reading. Put yourself in your guests' shoes and picture the kind of reception, amenities and other courtesies you would expect to be offered. Do the same for your guests.

Apart from these essential amenities, what gives the room a character are touches like fresh flowers, judiciously chosen books, and pictures on the wall.

Levels of Hospitality

Besides providing your guests with three basic meals a day, several refreshments in between must be offered. But whatever level of hospitality is planned, it should be within the financial capacity of the household. No inordinate strains should be put on resources of time, money and energy.

Do not get hysterical over small lapses on your part. You should always remember that it is you that your guests have come to visit, not some paragon of perfection or to judge your housekeeping standards.

It would be thoughtful to ask the guests before they go to bed whether they would appreciate an early morning cup of tea. If they are late risers, try and make as little noise as possible in the morning. If your maid goes away for the day finishing her work early, then you can either request her to do the guestroom during the daytime or else, a day or two later, you may put in a word casually to your guests. Good chances are that he will be up early the next morning, making life easier for you and your maid.

Although you can prepare some special dishes for your guests, do not tie yourself to cooking alone. Leaving your guests to their own devices all day long is bad manners. Remember he has come to visit you, not judge your culinary expertise.

Outings

Outings are a must. Take your guests out and show them places in and around your city. Arrange some shopping trips. It is courtesy that you should pay during all the outings unless your guests insist on picking up the tab. On personal shopping trips, it is okay for them to make the payment.

Presents
In all probabilities, your houseguest will bring something for you and your children. So it is your duty, as courtesy demands, to return their favours. If you cannot afford an expensive gift, a homemade gift such as bottles of pickles etc. can be given as a return gift to them.

Children
If your guests have small children with them, ensure an increased supply of milk for the duration of their stay. Remember to put away safely all your valuable art pieces and breakable show pieces so that no damage can be done and hence no hard feelings occur between you and your guests.

You as a House Guest
There are certain rules a house guest should always keep in mind:

*   In case your host has planned to put you up with his kids, don't make a fuss. It is not your home, so don't expect similar comforts here. Try to be as accommodating as possible.

*   If you or any member of your family has any food taboos or any other specific requirements, let the host know in advance.

*   Do not carry your pets with you.

*   Do not invite all your relatives and friends to meet you at your host's house. It is better to go to their houses to meet them or at a restaurant.

*   Do not try to discipline or criticize the host's children, no matter what they do. At the same time, do not ignore them either.

*   If your own children are very naughty, it is very imporant to keep a check on them to avoid unpleasantness with your host.

Offer to Help
Do not leave your room looking as though a hurricane has just

passed through. If the host does not have domestic help and they do their own housework, you are expected to at least make your own bed, offer to help in preparing meals, setting and clearing the table and even in washing dishes and clothes.

Do not inflict your help in certain areas as it may sometimes be a hindrance rather than a help to the host. Chances are that the host will have to redo your efforts.

The best way to keep yourself busy without coming in the host's way is by doing odd chores around the house, like watering the plants, taking the children to a nearby park and leaving your hostess free for some time to relax and finish her work peacefully. Offer to do the marketing for vegetables, groceries too.

Gifts

Always carry a souvenir for the host. It should be handed over at the first given opportunity or soon after opening your bags. It not only shows your thoughtfulness but also conveys a certain warmth in the relations.

The gift, however, should not be too expensive because in all probabilities, your host would like to reciprocate your gesture and if he is not that well off, your expensive present may leave him in a fix.

Bathroom Strategies

When hosts and guests share the same bathroom, some problems are bound to crop up. It would be kind, if the host gives his guest as much priority as possible in using the bathroom. However, do not take it as your right to use the bathroom first, specially if your host is in a hurry to go to office, or his children are rushing off to school.

It is acceptable, if the host has office- or school- going persons, who have to get ready at a certain time, to let the guest know about the morning rush hours. The guest, on his side, should also keep away from the bathroom around that time. After all, the whole day is ahead—what's your hurry? Remember, it is you who've come on a visit, not them. So don't make them feel restrained in their own house.

Children

Keeping your children in check is very important. It is your responsibility to make sure that they behave themselves. Do not permit them to be unruly or very demanding. Do not expect your host or hostess to run after your children and keep a check on their activities; it may prove to be a very trying and exasperating task. So instruct your children beforehand as to how to behave at the new household. Admonish them not to throw tantrums or fuss too much. Make sure they eat whatever is placed on the table. They may be fussy eaters at home, but must learn to eat whatever is cooked at another house.

See to it that your children do not get involved in fights with your host's children. Even if they do, restrain from making an issue of it even if you know that the other party is at fault. Above all, do not take the matter to their parents and demand an apology. Remember, children are innocent and open-hearted. One moment they fight and in a split second they are together, everything forgotten. Be tactful when settling children's disputes.

Remember, if you expect hospitality, reciprocate it with love, affection and extra care from your side.

Misuse of the Telephone

One of the most common evils houseguests are guilty of is misusing the telephone. Far worse than keeping their telephone busy the whole day with all those local calls, making lengthy long-distance calls at your host's expense is abominable.

Even if you have to make a call, keep it short and offer to pay for it. That your host may not accept it is another matter altogether.

Tipping Servants

At a house with domestic help, the appropriate time to tip those servants who have helped to make your stay agreeable is at the end of the visit. All the servants should be tipped equally. Tips should always be handed over in cash, with a word of thanks for services provided. If any of the servants is absent, it would be thoughtful to leave his share with the hostess. Before tipping, talk to the hostess and discuss the amount. Even if you are very rich, you cannot give a tip that is more than the servant's monthly salary.

Thanks
Guests should always write a note of thanks to the host on reaching back home. A simple thank-you card would also suit the purpose. Don't forget to mention how much you enjoyed the visit. Another appropriate gesture of thanks would be to send your hostess a bouquet of flowers.

TELEPHONE MANNERS

Tring, tring.

"Hello."

"This is ABC Refrigerator. Is your referigerator running?"

"No, it is very much in the same place as it has been standing for the past six years. Ha, ha, ha!"

Slam ... click.

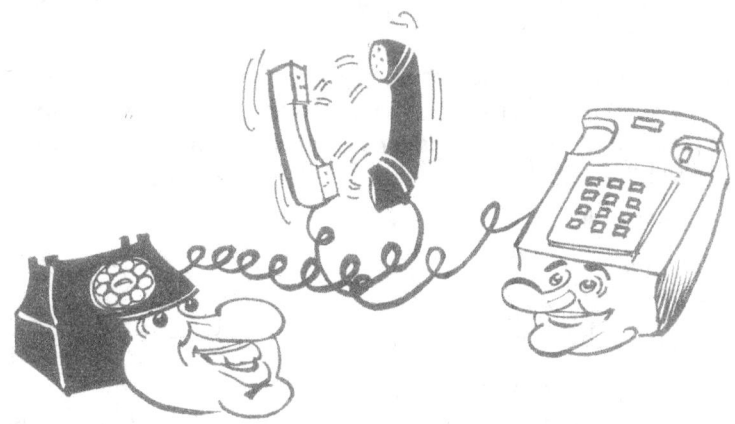

Timing

As a general rule, telephone calls to a household should not be made before 7 A.M. and after 11 P.M. However, there are many exceptions to the rule, depending upon who's calling whom and if it is an emergency.

Answering the Phone

A commonly accepted way of answering the phone is 'Hello'. In fact, that is all that needs to be said, but some like to announce their telephone number or their name as in '...6415911' or 'Sharma here'.

Staff in a big household sometimes announce the name of the residence quite like in an office:

'Burman House, Good Morning.'

In an office, it is customary to first greet the caller and then tell the name of the company. As soon as the telephone operator picks up the phone, she is expected to say:

"Good morning, Pasupati Acrylon", or "Good afternoon, Modi Rubber."

This way the caller knows he has dialled the correct number and he can immediately come to the point.

Identification

Announce your identity as soon as you know you have got through to the correct number.

If it's a personal call, you are likely to be familiar with all the family members. So ask after the well-being of the person on the line and then go on to ask for whomever you wish to speak to. The conversation will probably be as follows.

Receiver—"Hello."

You—"Is that 2415673?"

Rec.–"Yes."

You—"I'm Ruchika this side. May I know who's on the line?"

Rec.–"Hi Ruchika. I'm Radha."

You—"Hello Didi (since you know Radha is your friend's elder sister) How are you?"

Radha—"Fine, thank you. And how are you? Haven't seen you for a long time."

You—"Yeah, just busy with the studies. Didi, how is Reema? Is she around?"

Radha—"Yeah, yeah, she is here. I'll just call her, hold on for a minute."

She calls her younger sister with whom you can then chat.

Returning Calls

If the telephone call is mistakenly cut off, whoever made the call in the first place should call back. In case you were out or not free to speak at that particular moment and the caller leaves a message for you, then it is your duty to return the call.

Wrong Number

If you have dialled a wrong number (which happens very often) do not slam the phone down. You should apologize to whoever answered the call. If you answer the phone, and it is a wrong number, do not be rude. Just tell the caller "Sorry, you've got the wrong number" politely and ring off. If you persistently get wrong calls, do not take your frustration out on the other party. Instead, either ask the telephone exchange to get you the number or put the phone down and wait for some time before trying again.

Similarly, if you are at the receiving end of wrong numbers, tell them politely for the first few times, or else keep your phone off the hook for a few minutes. This may help the caller get the correct line, and you some peace.

Messages

Good message-takers are a boon to any office. The proper way of taking a message is by writing down the name of the caller, his number and the message clearly and accurately on a piece of paper. Leave this message where the recepient is most likely to see it.

Long Conversations

They are better avoided. Not only does it increase your telephone bill, it may also be an inconvenience to other people who are trying to get through to you, perhaps with an urgent message.

Ending a Phone Conversation

Even if both of you are great talkers, one has to tire first. Ideally, the best way is to wait for a pause in the flow and say something like:

'Sorry dear, but I have to cut it short ...'.

With some acceptable excuse like guests have come or the doorbell is ringing or the child is crying. Don't slam down the receiver on the caller when he is speaking. It is the height of rudeness. After you have conveyed your inability to continue the conversation, say 'I'll call you again soon' or 'Give me a call sometime'. This should be followed by the customary 'Bye, bye' or 'Be good, hope to see you soon' etc. This could be a definite indication of the end of a conversation.

Children on the Phone

Children love the telephone. The ringing of the phone is fascinating for a child. But this habit should not be encouraged. Unless your child is old enough to hold a conversation and take down the message, he should not be allowed to pick up the phone. At the same time, give him the occasional chance to converse over a phone in your presence. Teach him how to hold a conversation such as how to say hello, your telephone number, calling the concerned person and taking down the message. Slowly and gradually, he will master the technique.

Do not allow him to misuse the telephone. Picking up the receiver unnecessarily or dialling aimlessly, punching out numbers at random or stretching the cord around will not only damage the instrument but also keep your line engaged unnecessarily.

Answering Machine

Answering machines are the latest fad in our country and are gaining popularity because of their various uses. An answering machine is a device attached to the telephone instrument like an audio cassette and is used to record telephone messages in your absence.

All that you have to do is to switch on the machine before going out. If someone calls in your absence, they will be answered by a recorded message: "This is K. Mehta's residence. He is not at home right now. Please leave a message after the beep." The caller is now supposed to leave the message.

Try to be as brief as possible while talking to an answering machine. Just leave your name, call-back number and urgency of the matter on the tape. With an answering machine, you can be sure that the message will be received accurately.

WRITTEN COMMUNICATION

The moment we speak or write a few lines, it reveals more of ourselves than we may care to admit. Since the use of language is one of the chief yardsticks by which people evaluate others, we must try to be as much in command of our personal communication system as possible.

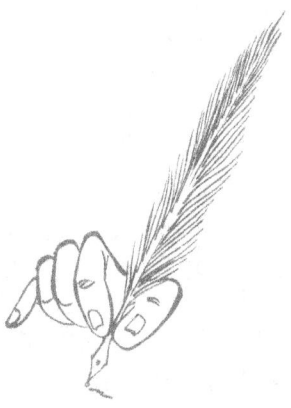

*O*ur written communication reveals as much of ourselves as our spoken words: "A letter is simply talk upon paper." As this is one of the chief yardsticks by which people evaluate us, you should try to be well in command of your personal communications system. Written communication is a matter of common courtesy and you should be concerned about how your method and manner of communication will affect others.

When you write a letter, you enter into a personal relationship with the reader. Now it is up to you whether you turn it into a jubilant, warm and friendly one or make it dull and dreary.

Is Writing a Chore?

Neither writing nor reading a letter should be viewed as a chore. Reluctant correspondents, to whom the art of letter-writing does not come naturally, will find their task easier if they work out what they want to say and how they wish to say it, before attempting to write a letter.

Letter Writing Formula

Simple and clear : The secret of writing a good letter lies in its being simple and clear. Just like one friend talking to another, a letter should sound like a good conversation. It should be straightforward, meaningful and written with a fixed purpose.

Salutation: The greeting to the reader with which every letter begins is called the salutation.

In a business or formal letter, it is

Dear Sir/Madam

If you want to give it a personal touch, write

Dear Miss Gandhi/ Mr Juneja

Never use 'Respected Sir/Madam' unless you are writing to a high dignitary or perhaps to the principal of your school. In an informal letter, the salutation begins with 'Dear' or 'My dear...' followed by the first name of the person, e.g. My dear Manoj or Dear Radha.

Making a good impression: The impression a letter makes on the reader depends on presentation as well as on content. Spelling and grammar should be watched, but in most private correspondence, a natural and personal flow of words is preferable. Faulty spelling is not acceptable except for the most private correspondence. Crossing out and the occasional inkblot are also excusable only in personal letters.

A letter set out nicely in the middle of the page, with wide margins, is pleasing to behold. Sufficient space between the lines, which should be even, is also pleasing to the reader.

Try and be as legible as possible. If your writing is hard to decipher, rely on a typewriter. To lend a personal note to typewritten letters, you can write the opening 'Dear so -and-so' and sign off with a pen.

Signatures to all letters are in the writer's hand.

Body

The body of a letter is where business is conducted.

Business letter: In a business letter, which is quite brief (rarely longer than one page, while most limit themselves to one or two paragraphs), one should come to the point directly. It is always better to be straightforward than beat around the bush.

Please note that 'short' does not mean that you adopt a shorthand or telegraphic style, leaving all your prepositions out. For example:

"Recd ltr Dec. 8. Will advise no later than one week."

This will do for a telegram but not a letter. Even in today's fast-paced world, this method is not adopted in a letter. Be sure every sentence is complete in itself and logical.

In a business letter, if you are writing on behalf of your company, use the first person as 'we' but when you are responding to a business letter in your personal capacity, use 'I' wherever possible.

"We are in receipt of your letter of 25.6.92 wherein..." (corporate basis).

"I am in receipt of your letter..." (individual capacity).

Personal letter: The body of a personal letter can include anything, depending upon your relationship and what you wish to convey. There is no set formula or prescription in writing a personal letter. A few broad guidelines may be suggested.

A general way of starting a personal letter to the following.

Friend:
My Dear Sheela,

Hello, I hope this letter finds you in the pink of health and spirits....

Elders:
Respected chachaji,

Namaste,

Hope this letter finds you in the best of health and spirits... .

A child :
My dear Tinny Minny,

How are you ? I received your lovely card only yesterday. It was real sweet of you to remember my birthday....

Closure

In the last para of the letter, you may if you wish stress once again anything that you have already written. It should motivate the reader into doing what you want him to do. It should also contain your farewell and the hope of hearing from the other party.

The closure, like the salutation, is a matter of custom and a polite way of concluding a letter. Expressions used must suit the tone of the letter and match the salutations which will be based on the relationship between the parties. The closure must be simple.

Business: In a business letter, about the most formal closing ever used today is:

Thanking you,

Yours faithfully,

Sd
Name of person
Designation

There is no need to write the name of the company or its address if you are using the official letter head. (This is when you have been using 'we' all along on the corporate level.)

When you use the 'Dear Sir/ Madam' address, sign off as 'Yours faithfully'. In case you address the person by name as

'Dear Mr Sharma', sign off as 'Yours sincerely'. If writing a business letter in an individual capacity, and having used 'I' throughout the letter, the closing should be:

With best/kind regards,

Yours sincerely.

'Yours obediently' should be kept only for those sick-leave letters to your school principal.

Personal: A personal letter can have any closing remark, depending upon your relations with the person.

Friends and peers: With lots of love, Yours sincerely,

or

Bye-bye for now, hope to see you soon,

Use 'Yours lovingly' only in case you are writing to your parents.

Elder relatives: With kind regards/Your (nephew/niece or whatever the relation is). If you do not wish to spell out the exact relationship, just write *'Yours affectionately'* and sign your name below.

Elders to children: It's time to close the letter. Now be good, take care. Convey my regards to your mom and dad.'

Yours lovingly,

Chintu *mama* or Radhika *mausi*

Consistency: The salutations should match their closures:

Salutations	Closures	Remarks
Dear Sir/ Madam	Yours faithfully	A formal letter on behalf of the company using 'we'.
Dear Miss Ram	Yours sincerely	Informal business letter written between persons known to each other using 'I'.
My dear Radha	Yours lovingly	A personal letter.

Signature : Sign legibly on any letter. Although in a personal letter, you do not write the name and designation as such, in a business letter, full name and title of the signing authority along with the name of the company should be clearly mentioned. Your signature should always be handwritten and just above the place where your name has been typed.

```
Yours faithfully,
for Modi Rubber Limited

Sign
(Ashwani Singhal) Financial Controller
```

Model Letters

General Business Letter

The ABC Corporation,
Parliament Street,
New Delhi.

Dear sir,

We are in receipt of your letter no. xyz dated 3.4.89 regarding your enquiry about our products.

In this regard, please find enclosed a set of our brochures containing the latest price list et al.

Hope it meets your requirement.

Thanking you,

Yours faithfully,
DEF Corpn Ltd,

Sd/-

(A.M. Gill)
General Manager

Letter of complaint

The Area Officer
Mahanagar Telephone Nigam Ltd,
New Delhi.

Sub: Wrong billing to phone no…for an STD call no… made to Calcutta.

Kindly refer to your bill no… dated… raised on telephone no…. To my utter amazement, I realize that I have been wrongly billed for an STD call to Calcutta code no… telephone no… for an amount of Rs 560.

I would like to add that no such STD call was made by me to Calcutta and I am absolutely unfamiliar with the Calcutta number that appears in my bill. Under the circumstances, kindly look into the matter and rectify the error at your earliest.

Thanking you,

Yours faithfully,

Sd/-

(Name, address and telephone number of the applicant.)

Letter of congratulations

My dear Rohit,

Hope this finds you in the best of health and spirits. I must first of all congratulate you on your receiving the scholarship to Hungary for three years. I was always sure that your hard work would win you this prestigious scholarship and I am glad that your efforts have been suitably rewarded now.

With warm regards and best wishes,

Yours sincerely,

Sd/-
(Rahul Ghosh)

Letter declining an invitation

Dear Arpita,

Thank you very much for your invitation to dinner next Saturday. I would have loved to be there and meet all of you, but unfortunately, I will be in Calcutta around that time, so you must please excuse me.

Meanwhile, I sincerely hope that your dinner party will be a great success. Give my love to all.

Yours affectionately,

Sd/-
(Radhika Menon)

Condolence letters

When someone dies, a letter of sympathy should be dispatched to their nearest and dearest as soon as possible. Keep the tone light and direct. Phrases such as: 'We send our heartful sympathies', or 'Please let me know if there is anything I can do', or 'We send our fondest love and thoughts to you at this time,' may be used.

Try not to write of the dead person as 'passed on' or 'passed over'. Direct reference is the best. You can write of any special memories of the dead person that the reader would like to hear about, any tribute that can be paid to their work, character or efforts.

Addressing an Envelope

Size: The envelope should neither be too big nor too small. It should be befitting the size of the letter.

Accuracy: The name and address should be exact and do spell each word correctly. Try not to use abbreviations like Bldg, St, Ave, Rd, etc. The Pincode should be given for prompt delivery.

Legibility: If typing the address, there should not be any overtyping. But if it is handwritten, do so in bold letters so that it is clear and easily readable.

Styles: There are two styles of writing addresses—Indent and Block forms:

   Mr A.K. Srivastava

(Indented form where each line is written after leaving some space.)

Mr A.K. Srivastava

(Block style where all the lines start from the same point.)

Specifications or Confidential or Personal

The words Confidential or Personal must be typed on the upper left-hand corner of the envelope or in the centre above the name.

The term Personal implies that the letter is meant for the reader alone and is not to be opened by his/her secretary. If marked Confidential, then it can be dealt with by the secretary.

Postscript

P.S. written at the base of a letter stands for 'postscript' and contains the writer's afterthoughts. The use of P.S. is wholly acceptable in most private correspondence but not in formal or official correspondence. Nor is it acceptable in a letter of condolence.

Book post: This means that the letter is sent open and not closed.

Card only: This is stictly for greeting cards etc. and not letters or any other documents. The postal charges are also lesser than for a normal letter.

UCP, Regd AD and speed post: These are different postal signs for sending a letter. You get a stamped receipt for these letters from the Post Office. It ensures speedy and confirmed delivery of the letter.

Airmail: All letters going out of the country should be marked 'Airmail'. They are weighed separately at the Post Office and stamped accordingly.

JOB HUNTING

"Job hunting? Is it the same as in tiger-hunting?"

"No way. It is much more rough and tough".

*J*ust as holding down a job successfully often involves matters of etiquette, there are a number of conventions in applying for and getting a suitable job.

The Resume or Curriculum

What do I want to do?: Before applying for a job, you have to answer this difficult question. Sit down with a piece of paper and list the things you are proud to have achieved. Take a stock of your personal accomplishments and list your strengths and weaknesses. Leave the latter aside and concentrate on the better part of your personality, the strengths.

Once you are clear in your mind about the line of profession you wish to pursue, talk to those already in the field. Then make a curriculum or resume or biodata.

Remember this will be your advertisement for a potential job and should highlight your strenghts, merits and achievements.

Main points of a resume: A resume should be in the following form.

Name and Address: Your name and address should be stated at the outset in bold letters. Please put the address to which correspondence is to be directed. Also indicate a telephone number where you can be reached.

Father/Husband's Name: Write Mr or Shri before the name.

Date of Birth: It can either be in numerical form or in words, like 23.7.68 or 23rd July, 1968.

Educational Qualifications: This includes your academic degrees. It should be given in the reverse chronological order, stating first your last acquired degree and going backwards to the previous ones.

Professional Qualifications: If you have any professional qualifications, like a secretarial course or have done a computer course or a management diploma, all these come under this head.

Present Job and Previous Employments: Descriptions of the jobs you have held in the past and the present one should be given again in the reverse chronological order. Begin with current work experience, then go onto previous jobs. Be sure to state your present desgination and previous ones as well as job descriptions.

Extracurricular Activities: If you have been a good sportsperson, mention it separately. Any other activities like dramatics, stage shows, or NCC, etc. that you have been involved in can be mentioned here.

Hobbies: The basic difference between the former and hobbies is that the former is done on a large scale, while the latter is strictly for one's own pleasure and is done in one's leisure time.

Salary Expected: This is a negotiable clause and if it is your first or second job, leave this column out. At this stage, you require experience more than to bother about the salary.

References: Give one or two names of persons known to you who are well settled and in reliable positions and whom you know will render you good backing in case your future employer wishes to enquire about you from them.

Model Biodata

Name	:	A.S. Jain
Father's Name	:	Mr M.K. Jain
Date of Birth	:	19.9.67
Permanent Address	:	B-1/10, Mayur Vihar, New Delhi. Tel: 551234
Postal Address	:	251, Park Street, Calcutta, Tel: 4456219

Educational Qualifications	:	1. B.Com from Delhi University in the year... with I Division (aggregate may be given).
		2. XII ...
		3. X ...
Professional Qualification	:	1. CA...
		2. Six months' Computer Course...
Job Experience	:	1. The present job, with the name of the company, designation and nature of job....
		2. Previous job.... .
		3. Prior to the above... .
Extracurricular activities	:	1. Good in sports. Played hockey at district level. 2. Cricket...
Hobbies	:	Reading, writing, gardening.
Salary Expected	:	Negotiable.
References:	:	1. Mr. H.K. Mathur, General Manager, ABC Corpn, 126, Parliament Street, New Delhi-1
		2. ....

Do not give more than two or three references.

Applications

A clear, informative, well-presented letter asking for employment is definitely singled out from the usual run-of-the-mill applications.

In response to an advertisement: Keep the following in mind when replying to an advertisement.

* Ensure that if specific information is requested, you supply it.

* Check that the full name of the person to whom the correspondence is addressed is accurately spelt and also that you

have included their prefix and correct designation, such as the Personnel Director.

*   The address must be accurate.

Applying for a job when there is no advertisement: When you send an unsolicited letter, it is best to address your correspondence to a specific named individual and not an anonymous Head of a Department. Applications may be sent to the Managing Director or the Personnel Manager.

Content: A letter that accompanies your resume should state whether you are replying to an advertisement (state the publication and date) and produce an interesting reason why you think you should be considered for the post. Enthusiasm for the field, aptitude for the work and aspirations to succeed, along with relevant experience or qualifications are best.

Indicate whether you are currently employed/immediately available. Do not make any reference to your present contract of employment.

Use clean white paper and write only on one side of the paper.

To type or not: Job applications are usually typewritten, but in certain cases applicants are asked to write in their own hand.

Interview

Once you have sent your biodata with the application, if the management considers you suitable for the job, you will get a call letter to appear for the interview on a particular date, at a specific time.

Punctuality is important, but arriving noticeably ahead of time suggests lack of confidence and inexperience. So give not more than 10 minute's grace. At the same time, being late for an interview not only shows discourtesy, it is also a very poor start. Once at the reception desk, give your full name and the name of the person with whom you have the appointment or you can even show your call letter.

Making a good impression: Unfair as it may be, many hopes are won or lost in the first impression, a crucial factor. During the opening stages of the interview, it is better to respond than to initiate.

Greeting: If the interviewer extends his hands, shake it warmly, otherwise just say hello with a nod. Acknowledge a smile with a smile.

Posture counts: Enter the room gracefully with shoulders back, head high. Wait to be told where to sit, but if no guidance is forthcoming and you see a chair which you assume is for the interviewer, don't just go and dump yourself onto it. First ask: "May I sit here?" Then sit down.

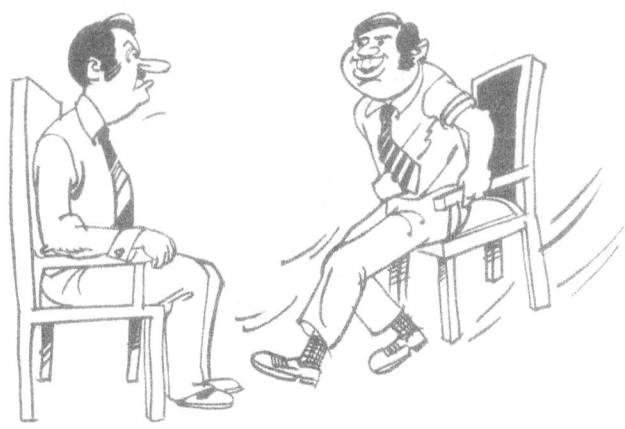

Incidentally, smoking during the interview, even if the interviewer has offered you a cigarette, is definitely out. Never ask if you may smoke.

Poise and grace: Do not look disturbed or try to avoid the issue when tough questions are put.

Maintain a natural eye-contact with the interviewer and try to control the often unconscious habit of staring aggressively or of looking down. Act and look totally at ease.

Carry all your credentials and certificates with you. Should the interviewer's telephone ring while he is not in the room, do not answer it.

Dress sense: Despite the general casualness, it is a sound practice to show yourself to your best advantage by taking the trouble to look good at a job interview.

Clothes which are good, sober, in which you feel relaxed and at ease and which suit you the best should be chosen for the occasion. Emphasize on depicting yourself as a well-groomed person.

Men: In summer, wear a full-sleeved shirt and tie, opting for a suit in winter.

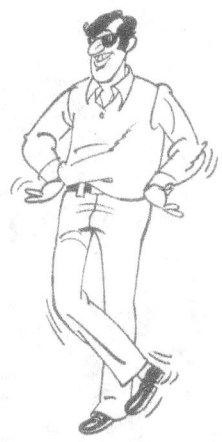

Ladies: Salwar kameez or saree are both acceptable and can be worn in all climatic conditions. Trousers are out.

In the Interview

Address the interviewers with their usual prefix, while avoiding repetitive use of their names—"Yes, Mr Sharma", "No, Mr Sharma".

Take care to inform yourself about the job and the company before the interview. If being interviewed by SAIL (Steel Authority of India Ltd), find out how many plants they have and where they are located. Prepare convincing answers to such questions as—Why are you interested in working for SAIL?; How do you see your career developing?; and Do you see yourself as an asset to the company and how?

Women who have young children at home may face inquiries about child-care arrangements and their adjusting to the demands of the job.

References/background : Always offer to supply references, giving name address and telephone of each person. Don't forget to get the prior permission of the person whose name you wish to give as a referee.

Redundancy: If you have been made redundant by a previous employer, describe the background to put yourself in the clear. If other members of the staff also suffered similarly, this may be used as supporting evidence.

Sacked: If you were previously sacked for alleged incompetence, you are under no obligation to mention the fact. But if your employer intends to take up references from your previous employer, use suitable explanations such as: misunderstandings about the nature of the job, a personality clash with the boss, being the victim of racist or sexist discrimination, a divorce in the family—these will prepare him in advance.

Do not speak ill of a previous employer in front of a prospective one. You will be earmarked as a disloyal person. Instead, indicate lessons that you have learned.

Rewards and Benefits

Once you are told that you are chosen for the job, you should always raise the topic of salary and conditions of work, if the interviewer seems slow in getting round to the point.

Do not give him the impression that your primary interest lies not in the job itself but in the wages and other benefits it offers, instead just inquire in a general way about these things.

Departure

When the interview is at an end, you should thank the interviewer for his time, shake hands and say good bye, maintaining an optimistic air throughout. It is okay to ask when you are likely to be informed of any decision.

Letter of Confirmation

Remember, at a certain level, the interviewers are looking for some-one with whom they can feel comfortable—a face that fits—so be cheerful, optimistic, enthusiastic and confident.

If you are successful, you will receive a letter of confirmation or a contract setting out terms and conditions. These should be very carefully perused before signing, as they often have legal clauses. Always keep a copy of any agreement or contract with you.

ETIQUETTE AT WORK

Give up your seat
The big boss will expect it
an 'I was here first'
Does not mark way
To future promotion
Big or small
The boss certainly does expect it.

*I*n the workplace, people are judged by criteria different from that which prevails outside. Efficiency, power, and success are the main goals. The gentleness that is associated with courtesy may be no match for success here—regrettable as this may sound, but this is the truth.

Most offices have their own way of doing things which can only be learned through observation and experience on the job. However, some general guidelines hold true for all times, like the principles underlying good manners, which do not change with the weather.

Office Code of Behaviour
Every office has its specific code of behaviour that includes the manners the employees exhibit to one another. So watch for a few days, then go along with it.

Too much formality, however, in an office that does not call for it, can make you look stuffy, whereas a lack of good manners towards fellow employees can make you dangerously unpopular. So maintain a balance and learn to survive.

First Name or Formal Style
Addressing staff members by their first names is a commonly

accepted practice, yet the formal style of using prefix and surname as in (Ms Jain) is still practised and can never be considered incorrect. So test the water before taking the plunge.

Much depends on the sector of employment also. Senior members of the office are addressed formally in a respectful way by those who are considerably junior in rank.

Telephone Tactics

The telephone is a double edged weapon—both a boon and a curse. Be polite and brief on the phone. Avoid personal calls as much as possible.

Team Play

Coordination between all the departments is very necessary so that the whole office can work as a team. It not only increases efficiency but inter-personal relationships also.

Handling Rivals

Aggressive and competitive rivalry exists in almost every office. And they can be very treacherous.

How to deal with them? Well, since you have already chosen to run a civilized race, it probably won't do you any good to try to beat such a rival at his own game. The best way out is to beat him at your own best game—good manners and fair play. Any dirty tactics the rival uses can be countered with a little presence of mind and polished manners. It is most likely that in front of his already established ill-reputation, your good manners will shine out and there, you've won the game.

Overcoming Malicious Gossip

Gossip is part of any office's informal channel of communication. The best way is to remain aloof from the gossipers without actually alienating yourself. Earn a reputation for not gossiping and at the same time keep alert to any gossip that may be interesting or helpful to you. Be perceptive so that you can know beforehand, in case some rumour concerning you is going around. Rumours may seem too petty a subject to be bothered about but sadly enough more than one career has been needlessly destroyed by a competitor spreading malicious gossip. So beware and be prepared.

When a damaging rumour is started, the best way to put an end to it is by confronting its originator as soon as possible and in public. Since you are going to handle this situation in a calm, polite, up-front manner and since there is little doubt about the other person's motives, you have nothing to lose and everything to gain by making the confrontation a public one. A well-mannered public confrontation might go like this:

You: "I heard you told our boss that I was planning to accept a new position with XYZ Corpn."

The gossipmonger (will probably just stutter, too embarrassed and taken aback by this sudden confrontation in public): "Well...".

You: "That's quite a piece of misinformation, isn't it?"

The g. (more stuttering): "I don't know. Is it? "

You: "It certainly is. I've straightened it out with our boss, and I hope you won't be repeating it any more."

End of exchange, end of rumour and no need for any further clarifications. You have already achieved what you wanted.

Helping Out a Colleague
It is considerate to offer help to an overworked colleague but not at the cost of your own work. Offer only when you have free time.

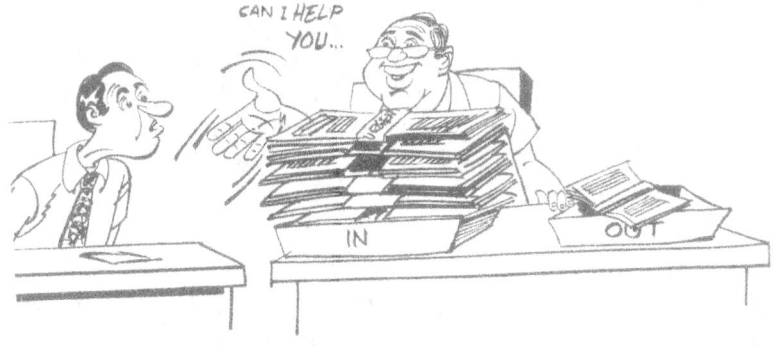

Also, do not earn the reputation of a universal do-gooder. Offer help only when necessary.

Do not brag about the help you have rendered to your colleague, it will give better effect if your colleague himself gives you due credit at an appropriate moment.

Managing Relations with Your Boss

It is very important to be in perfect harmony with your boss. For it is necessary to cater to his ego without going overboard. If your boss is good at his work and highly principled, he will not be particularly interested in having yes-people around. Even if he likes some flattery, do so graciously and within certain limitations. Remember even the largest ego knows when it is being played like a musical instrument.

Discuss your problems about work but never your personal problems. Do not let him see through your weakness. At the same time, do not promise more than what you can deliver.

Handling Subordinates when You have Just Become Boss

This is a tricky situation because till yesterday, you were one among them and today, all of a sudden, you are their senior. Treat them with grace and respect. You are likely to know their natures well. In fact, many of them may even have been your friends till you got promoted. Do not let your newfound authority go to your head and think you must maintain a stiff distance. At the same time, do not treat your friends like favoured people so that they are nicknamed your *chamchas*.

Be friendly, but don't be a pal now. Keep intimate friendships for after-office hours. Intimacy and friendliness are two different things. The former may find yourself in a binding situation which can be harmful to your ambitious career, while the other helps you in achieving further goals.

Handling a Dispute

Sooner or later, you may have a handle a dispute among subordinates. There is an art to doing so. First of all, do not play favourites. Insist that the two fighting employees treat each other with politeness and respect. Then listen to each person's story individually. Be sure to hear both sides. Treat both with the same respect and attention. One good ploy is to ask each person for a written memo detailing the aspects of the dispute. This will give you some breathing room. Also, it will force the arguing persons to confront the issue more directly.

Memos
An ideal office memorandum is short, to the point and civil in tone. Avoid any humorous references, irony or flippant remarks. An office memo should be dated and bear full names of the sender and receiver. A record should be kept of all the distributed memos.

Business Cards
The style of quiet restraint characterizing a visiting card is definitely more assertive in a business card. Business cards should have: the full name, person's designation, name and address of the company, telephone, fax and telex numbers and address in complete.

Office Parties
These are generally staid affairs to meet those in senior positions on informal grounds and encourage a more relaxed approach between the employers and employees.

Circulate: The host should welcome all the guests and then circulate around, saying appropriate things to each person. Punctuality from staff members is essential and they must not stick to one group but circulate.

While juniors must strike up contacts with their seniors, they should be careful not to monopolize an important person throughout the evening.

Women at parties: Even at parties, women must project a business-like image. Avoid taking up unwanted lifts home and enlist the help of your own sex to help you out a sticky situation. If you see a woman colleague trying to fend off unwanted flirtation or advances, be sure to help her out.

Drinks : Alcohol may be freely available but don't imbibe too much. An intoxicated person, be he a junior staff member or a manager, will find it difficult to face his colleagues the next day. An intoxicated male staffer may also incur the wrath of the female members in his organization.

Love in the Office

The working environment affords endless opportunities for romance and marriage, not necessarily in that order. For those unattached people on the lookout for romantic attachments/ affairs, both of which may or may not lead to marriage, the modern office is a common meeting ground.

Rebuffs/Rejecting Advances

A woman may wish to rebuff unwanted attention but may feel constrained to do so, fearing that her job could be jeopardized or her work discriminated against.

How to do this: Responding to unwanted attention requires a cool head, tact and a reliance on good humour. Avoid puncturing a man's vanity, particularly if he is the boss. Instead, put him off by light frivolous conversation or a stern dismissive glance can also convey more than words.

One thing is to be remembered — romance, affairs may develop at the workplace but flaunting a relationship in office must be avoided at all costs.

Men must remember that sexual innuendos and crude remarks (sometimes in reference to a particular woman colleague) must be out of a woman's hearing. It is an insult to your colleague if you do this.

HAPPY OCCASIONS: BIRTHS AND ANNIVERSARIES

The famous poet T.S. Eliot, surely had humans in mind when he wrote his famous verses about the nomenclature of cats:

'The naming of cats is a difficult matter.'

It isn't one of your holiday games.

At first you may think I'm mad as a hatter when I tell you a cat must have THREE DIFFERENT NAMES

The same goes for most of us: the scientific name, the domestic name and the pet name.

*B*irths, naming ceremonies, anniversaries, and marriages are occasions for joy, happiness and cheer.

Births

People of different religions and communities have their own unique birth rites and ceremonies but the common factor among them is the aura of happiness accompanying each occasion.

If you are invited to participate in a function for a child's birth, it would be a good idea to acquaint yourself with these rites and ceremonies. India being such a vast secular country, it is not an easy task to do so with each and every one. So the best way out would be to observe the others present and ape them.

Hindus: Generally all those belonging to the Hindu community perform a *havan* on the sixth day after the child's birth, called *Chhatti,* and later a naming ceremony called *Namkaran Sanskar.* Both the functions are presided over by a *Pandit,* who performs the *havan* and other rituals and in the end, everyone blesses the baby.

Muslims: *Berit Milah* is the first rite for an infant male child. He is circumsized when eight days old. The religious ceremony is attended by parents, grandparents and close friends. Prayers and blessings are heaped on the infant and celebrations take place. But someone appropriately said 'Like all great ceremonies in life, the *Berit Milah* is also designed to be enjoyed by everyone except the guest of honour (the baby).'

A ceremony called *Kathe Koran* takes place at the age of 12 when the child is made to read from the holy *Koran*.

Sikhs: Instead of a *havan*, they take the child to the gurdwara. An *Akhand Path* may be organized, and the child is blessed by Shri *Guru Granth Sahib* and holy water. *Prasad* is distributed and this may be followed by a feast.

Christians: Christians hold a ceremony called 'Baptism'. A child may be baptized at any age, but the rite usually takes place sometime between the age of six weeks and four months.

During the ceremony, the child's parents, grandparents and other relatives bring the child to the baptismal font in the Church. The priest asks the parents to 'name their child'. Besides the natural parents, two other people are invited to be there as godparents. The priest then sprinkles the water on the baby's forehead and pronounces its name. It is a brief ceremony after which everyone may be invited to a party at the parents' home.

Naming the Child
Naming the newborn is a bundle of considerations. First of all, there is the name that is given as per the horoscope. Second is the official name by which the child is known, e.g. Rahul Sharma. The third might be kept affectionately within the family.

Presents for Mother and Child
The best choice on this occasion is something for the baby, like a dress, toy or if you want to give something more expensive, maybe a baby cot or pram, etc.

However, the proud new father and the grandparents might choose to bestow a more substantial gift which helps to secure the financial security of the child, like some share certificates, NSCs, Indira Vikas Patra, a bank FD, Units or something in the form of jewelry can be given.

Though all attention is focussed on the newborn, thoughtful friends and family members should remember the mother too. It would be kind to produce a present just for her, such as a bottle of perfume, a book on childcare, a saree, etc. Rest assured, the gesture will be noted with much gratitude.

Conduct during the Ceremonies

Imagine the plight of the little one who has just entered this jungle of human beings. All of a sudden after being cocooned for nine months, it finds itself in the midst of hordes of odd creatures (the near and dear ones, of course) descending upon him, touching, making faces or merely staring at him. The 'ga gaas, goo goos' and 'cluck, clucks' should be minimized or preferably reserved for a later visit. When the touching and poking carries on for far too long, the baby itself finds a simple solution to chase everybody away by screaming its head off.

So it is better to just pay your good wishes to the parents.

Birth of a Girl Child

One glaring social evil is the stigma that is attached to the birth of a girl. Guests, instead of congratulating the parents, are found consoling them. And this is more so if it is the second or third daughter. For a new father or mother, a child whom she has reared for nine months in her womb is dear, no matter what its sex.

So keep your ideas to yourself and instead of consoling them, give them your best wishes.

Some Choice Phrases

There are certain standard phrases that can be used on these occasions:

"Congratulations, what a lovely baby!"

"Congratulations, you really took your own time, but it's worth it" (If the child is born after a long time after marriage)

"Congratulations, and how are you feeling now?" (In case it's a caesarian delivery)

"Congratulations. What have you named her/him?"

"Good, now your family is complete." (In case, it is their second child.)

Birthdays

Nothing else pleases a person more than the fact that someone has remembered his/her birthday. Courtesy demands that we wish those we love and respect, on their birthdays.

Often, it may not be possible to personally greet everyone. Hence, it is customary to send a birthday card well in advance. Also, even if you can't visit them, making a phone call on the day will serve the same purpose.

A word of caution : everyone's memory has a quaint habit of playing tricks, hence maintaining a diary of birthdays and anniversaries is an excellent idea. Nowadays, the postal authorities have introduced greeting telegrams, but that sounds and feels too general. The thought, the looking around, the trouble you take in finding a good card is all that goes into and makes a card worthwhile, which is obviously absent in sending a greeting telegram.

Anniversaries

A similar code of conduct applies to anniversaries. Wedding anniversaries in particular, offer another opportunity of greeting our near and dear ones. An anniversary card, a bouquet or a small gift can make the couple's day.

They, on the other hand, as is customary these days, throw a party inviting close friends and relatives. A cake is cut by the couple, followed by the dinner. In general, anniversaries are classified as follows:

> 10 years — Copper anniversary;
> 20 years — China anniversary;
> 25 years — Silver annivarsary;
> 30 years — Pearl anniversary;
> 35 years — Coral anniversary;

40 years — Ruby anniversary;
45 years — Sapphire anniversary;
50 years — Golden anniversary;
55 years — Emerald anniversary;
60 years — Diamond anniversary; and
65 years — Platinum anniversary.

FOR SAD OCCASIONS: DEATHS AND FUNERALS

A long, long time ago,there was an old lady who had a son. She loved him more than her own life. One day, unfortunately, the son died. The woman went mad with sorrow. She had heared a lot about Lord Buddha and his eternal powers. She went up to him and begged for her son's life.

Seeing her state, Lord Buddha took mercy on her and told her "If you bring a handful of soil from that house where no one has ever died, I will bring your son back to life."

The woman ran back gleefully to do so as she was told. But everywhere she went, she was faced with disappointment. There was not a single house in the whole village which had never experienced death. Now the old lady realized the futility of her efforts. She came to terms with the reality of life, the law of nature.

*Y*es, however painful it may be, death is inevitable. The loss of a mother, father, brother, sister, husband, or wife or any near and dear one is the most severe form of psychological stress. Yet, unfortunately, sometime or the other, everyone has to undergo it. At other times, we might have to comfort and console our bereaved friends and relatives. Such is life. Personal grief might find its outlet in tears. But it is only after the initial shock is over, that the void left behind begins to hurt and the realization dawns that you will never be able to see that person in this lifetime. Indeed, the pain of grief is as much a part of life as the joy of love. It is perhaps the price we pay for love.

The Inevitable and the Immediate Chores

Once the inevitable has struck, the person closest to the deceased is hard hit. Since the time is so heavy for him, he is treated in much the same way as a person who has fallen ill. His near and dear ones take over the responsibility of making decisions on his behalf. The immediate and most important chore is to inform relatives near and afar, friends, business or office colleagues and others close to the deceased about the tragedy.

This is followed by a number of formalities to be fulfilled in the form of: registration of death, obtaining a death certificate, releasing obituary notices in the newspaper, arranging religious services, calling the undertaker, and intimating the authorities at the crematorium.

Conduct

Formalities are determined by the priest or religious leader but mourning in itself is a private matter. There is no set pattern for an individual's conduct on an occasion such as a death, since so much depends upon each individual's relationship with the deceased.

Condolences

After paying homage to the deceased, as a custom, everyone offers their sympathy to the immediate members of the family. This custom was started to cushion their initial shock by the sympathy of well-wishers who visit the bereaved family and join them in their time of grief. These visits and expressions of sympathy are appreciated by the bereaved family members. These are accepted as a tribute to the dead person and at the same time, they also reassure the bereaved that they are not alone in the world.

For most of the time, you are likely to find yourself at a loss for words as to what to say to the bereaved family members. No words seem appropriate and no matter what you say, it will not lessen their grief. For one thing, always speak with your heart. There should not be a hollow ring to what you say. Be genuine, if you really feel for them and want to be of any help. If you can't manage it truthfully, it is better to keep quiet and just hug the person close, clasp hands or make similar gestures which convey your feeling for them.

It often happens that only those who share the grief or those who themselves have suffered a loss in the past feel for the bereaved family genuinely.

At the Funeral of an Old Relative

If you are attending an old person's funeral, it is quite likely that you will either have to pay your condolences to his wife or the children.

Don't sound casual or try to be little the loss. If you are a relative or a close friend, try to stay with the bereaved family for a couple of days to provide them moral support. Do not start discussing personal and financial matters then and there. If at all you have to say something to the bereaved family, then say something sensible like:

'At least he lived a full life', or 'He didn't have to suffer much in his last days', etc. This may ease the pain.

At the Funeral of a Young Person

This is a very painful tragedy for family members as well as close friends. Even a mere acquaintance will, on hearing about such a death, stop by to share the grief.

If you are an immediate relative or intimate friend, give the bereaved family moral, emotional as well as financial support (if necessary). Try to be as helpful as you can by bringing food if you live close. Since they have lost the one who used to look after all the work around, they will be needing as many hands and as much sympathy as possible. Offer your car to them for a day or two if they have no transport. A genuine 'I'm sorry' and other gestures of help will earn you the undying gratitude of the bereaved family. Never start discussing future plans for the spouse of the dead.

Telling parents to find solace in their next child is of no use. They already know that but at the same time, they also know that no one can take their deceased child's place, not even their second or third child.

At the Funeral of a Child

The funeral of a child under three years is slightly different—different in performing rites as well as the atmosphere. Since the child has not had ample opportunity to move around socially except for close relatives, others do not feel particularly attached to him.

The prevailing thought on such occasions is: 'So what if one child died. They are still young. They can have another one.' But don't you ever dare voice such ideas to the parents. Ask that crying mother or that silently mourning father—can anyone ever replace their sweet little one who is now just a memory? No, not even their second child can replace what this child gave them. Only fond memories can revive him in their thoughts. So on such occasions just say, 'I'm very sorry about it. What actually happened to the baby?' or 'How did this happen?'

In the Business Circle
If it's a close associate, visit the place and offer your help.

In case you are unable to pay a personal visit, send a condolence telegram addressed to the eldest member of the family :

'Very sorry to hear about the sad demise of... May his Soul rest in peace. May the Almighty give strength to all of you to bear this irreparable loss.' This can be followed by a letter offering any kind of help.

Dress
Bright colours are to be absolutely avoided at a funeral. Gaudy dresses, lipsticks, heavy jewelry, trendy hairstyles are for parties, not for funerals. You should look, wear and act sober. Maybe that is the reason why, in our country, white is the colour of mourning. Ladies wear white sarees and men white *kurta-pajama* or *dhoti*.

In some cultures, where white is not worn by married ladies, they can wear cream, beige or any other sober colour so long as it matches the mood and atmoshpere. Christians wear black, grey or brown at funerals, not white.

Children
As far as possible, avoid taking children to funerals. Not only because

children being children will not understand the seriousness of the situation and will run around playing and demanding everyone's attention but also for psychological reasons. Seeing death at a young impressionable age can adversely affect a child. This may not only give rise to several questions in a child's curious mind but make him scared too.

So it is better to leave children at home. If the tragedy has occurred in your own house, leave the kids either with one of your relatives or with neighbours where they can be looked after properly, fed on time and kept away from the mourning atmosphere.

However, do explain to your child what death is and explain that aunty or uncle has gone away forever or has been called by God.

Letter of Condolence

In case it is impossible to pay your last respects to the deceased, a letter which is short and written with restraint should promptly be dispatched to the immediate members of the family.

It is of great importance to write promptly and with sincerity. Be brief. The purpose of a letter of condolence is to console the living. Avoid harping on the tragic aspects of the death but refer to the happy memories and good done during the deceased person's lifetime (already explained in the chapter Written Communication).

Acknowledging Letters of Condolence

Nobody expects an immediate reply to a condolence letter.

In case there is a large number of letters of condolence, a classfied advertisement of thanks can be relased in the newspaper. Members of the intimate circle, however, need to be thanked individually. Others may be sent a printed card as acknowledgement.

DILEMMAS

'She loves me. She loves me not.'

He kept on breaking pretty petals of the lovely lily flowers.

Though she couldn't have started loving him just because the last petal fell on 'She loves me', it somehow helped him. It ceased his dilemma.

*T*here are some embarassing moments in our lives—a time comes when we find ourselves in a fix. At such moments, although we know something has to be done, we are not quite sure what exactly.

At a Party

☆ **What should you do if you are served a dish at a party that gives you an allergy?**

Nobody should feel obliged to eat food that is a health hazard to him. It is best to decline the dish, mentioning the fact.

☆ **If the host is not looking, should you help yourself to another drink from the bottle?**

If the drinks are being served by a waiter—help yourself. But if the host himself is serving the drinks, it is impolite to go and pour the drink out yourself.

☆ **If you are seized by a coughing fit during the meal, what should you do?**

Try not to panic. Ask for a glass of water quickly. If you feel nauseous, immediately get up and and head towards the bathroom. Stay there for a short while till you recover your composure and then return to the company.

☆ *How do you indicate you have finished your meal ?*

Put the knife and fork together in the centre of the plate. But when you pause in between the mouthfuls, set them slighly apart, indicating that you are not yet done.

☆ *You have invited a friend who turns out to be an alcoholic, knocking back peg after peg. What should you do?*

Make his drinks as light as possible. Announce an early dinner which will effectively stop the drinks supply. And do not call him to your party next time.

☆ *How long should you keep dinner waiting for a very late guest?*

Give this particular guest a grace time of about an hour and a half. If you still haven't heard from him, go ahead and start the dinner. It is not fair to the other guests.

☆ *Your child is bent on destroying an intricate decoration at a party—what should you do?*

Stop him from doing so immediately but quietly. If he does not listen, take him away from there and try to distract him quietly. Shouting at him or hitting him in front of everyone should not be done as it not only attracts unnecessary attention, but also makes the host feel guilty and finally spoils the fun of the party.

☆ *You know that a certain guest has stolen a piece of silverware from the table. What should you do?*

If a child has done it, take him aside and point out the error of his ways. He will return it. But if an adult has done it, let the issue pass for the time being. At a later date, speak to that person about the incidence, giving someone else's reference. He will get the hint. Although he cannot return that piece now (out of sheer embarrassment) but rest assured he will not repeat the act. At least not in your house.

☆ *You have invited a guest to your party who does not eat onions and by mistake you forgot to inform your cook. All the dishes are prepared with onions and garlic in them.*

The best way to rectify your mistake is by utilizing that period when drinks are being served. Cook up two-three simple dishes like fried potatoes, a *raita*, etc., which are without onions.It is better to have just one or two simple dishes of that person's taste rather than not having a single dish, with the result that you end up apologizing profusely and repeatedly.

☆ **Your host has offered you tea which you do not drink at all.**

If you do not drink tea for health reasons, decline it. If it is just that you are not particularly fond of it, take a few sips, then quietly push the cup under the trolley.

☆ **You are invited to a cocktail party but you do not drink.**

Preferably decline the invitation as you are likely to feel out of place there. If you can't, then go ahead and accept soft drinks. Still, if someone insists on your having at least one drink, do not sound too rigid by saying a strict no, take the glass and while away the whole evening without actually drinking it. Seeing your full glass, no one will offer you another drink.

Children

☆ **At a children's party, should the return gifts be given to parents also?**

There is no need to give presents to parents separately. If you want to pay them back for their expensive gifts, instead give presents to the kids.

☆ **If your nine-month-old baby is being invited to a birthday party in the neighbourhood, what should you do?**

Since everyone knows that a small child cannot move around on his own, it is but obvious that someone has to accompany him—most likely the mother. So do not feel embarrassed—it is understood that when they invited your baby, they expect you to come with the child.

☆ **Two children are fighting at your child's birthday party. Should you scold them or send them back home?**

None of the above. First try to stop them. If they still go on, be firm and make them sit apart from each other. Do not slap even shout at them. Remember, they are your guests.

☆ **Your son's teacher is being partial towards some students, with the result that he starts hating the school. What do you do?**

Talk to the teacher and try to make her/him understand how her/his behaviour is affecting your son. But if she still persists in her favouritism or on the other hand becomes harsh with your son, then take matters up to the Principal and leave it in his hands. If nothing works, it is better to change the school.

☆ *You go to an elderly relative's house where shoes are left at the front door. You, however, were not aware of the custom. It was only after entering and having seated youself comfortably that you notice that everyone else is not wearing shoes.*

The best way would be to apologize, saying that you were not aware of this custom. Then go out and remove your shoes.

☆ *You receive a letter from some relatives informing you of their visit to your house for a few days' stay. You have already made a programme for an outing and made all the reservations. What should you do?*

If the guests are from the close family, like your parents, in-laws, etc., you can either cancel your programme or if you can afford it and feel it appropriate, make reservations for them also to go with you. If what you have planned for yourself is unavoidable and at the same time it is not possible to take your guests along, then inform them immediately about your programme. Apologize and request them to alter their plans till after you come back from your trip.

☆ *You meet some relatives from your in-laws' side at a party, should you touch their feet in public?*

Our traditional form of greeting elders is by touching their feet. So there is no harm in doing so even at public places. Of course, if that person himself feels embarrassed and stops you from doing so, that's another matter.

☆ *At a party, someone extends his hand for a handshake while you being from a very conservative family do not appreciate such behaviour. Should you turn away or shake hands nevertheless?*

Well, none of these. That's his manner of greeting you, so you reciprocate in your own way. Fold your hands instead and say *namaste*. Don't worry, he won't be any more offended than you are.

Eating Out

☆ *You have gone to a restaurant where you find the service is very poor. Calling the waiter is very difficult. What can you do?*

Try attracting the waiter's attention in a decent and polite manner. Do not shout. If you find that he is deliberately avoiding you, go to the manager and complain. If even the manager does not take notice, leave in protest and go to another restaurant.

☆ *You have seen the waiter dipping his finger in your finger bowl before bringing it to you. You do not like it. What do you do?*

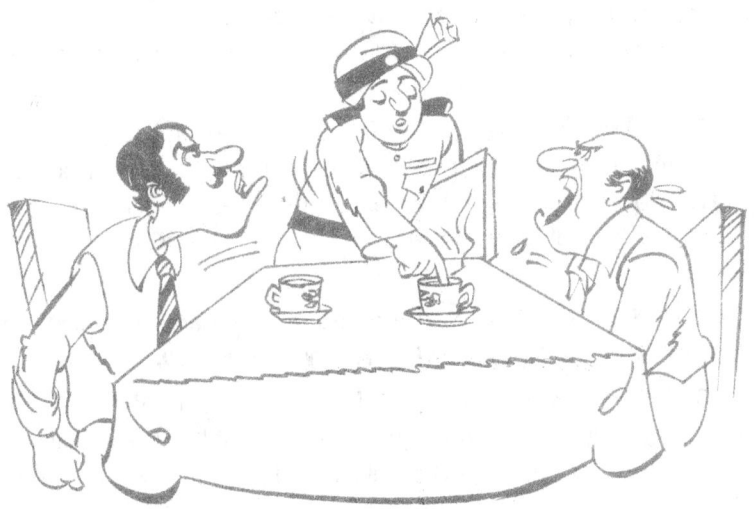

Shouting or creating a scene is not good manners. As soon as the waiter has placed the finger bowl in front of, say politely, 'Have you checked the temperature properly? I hope your finger is not burnt.' Then go on to tell him politely to change all the bowls. Don't worry, he will be too embarrassed to give you dirty looks.

☆ *You go to an expensive restaurant for lunch with a not-too-rich friend. You want to pick up the tab, so as not to burden him financially. He, on the other hand, insists on paying the entire amount from his own pocket. What should you do?*

If you tell him straightaway that you want to pay because of his financial constraint, it will be an insult to him. Say something plausible such as you've been promoted so the treat is on you, etc. Don't make a mess of the whole thing by saying it is your birthday or marriage anniversary because if he knows the date, he will immediately see through the excuse. On the other hand, he may end up buying you a present much more expensive than the cost of the lunch.

Travelling

☆ *You have entered your train compartment in a hurry and knocked over someone's water pitcher. Of course, it broke. The traveller is a lady with two small children. What should you do?*

Apologize profusely and offer to buy her another one. If the train is moving, share your water with her and buy her a water bottle or a pitcher at the next stop. If she wishes to pay for the bottle herself, refuse as it was your fault that it broke in the first place.

☆ *You have gone to see a movie and the person behind you is constantly talking loudly and disturbing you.*

Tell him politely a few times. If he still does not listen, see if you can shift to any other empty seat in the hall. If none is available, try to concentrate harder on the film, maybe it wasn't your day.

At Work

☆ *Your boss who is otherwise very nice is very short-tempered at times. One day he shouts at you in front of a group of visitors. You feel humiliated. What will you do?*

Talk it over with him privately after the visitors have left. Let him realize you also have self-respect and he should not take you for granted.

Funeral

☆ *You have received an invitation for an engagement and are expected to attend a funeral ceremony on the same day and almost the same time. What do you do.*

Either you can split the invitation with your family like you attend the funeral, and your younger brother attends the engagement ceremony. You may, if you wish, explain the reason for the other person's absence. In case you both have to be present at both the places, leave the first place slightly early, go home, change quickly and reach the other function slightly late. Changing in between is very necessary as you cannot wear the same clothes to both the functions, since one is a happy occasion and the other sad.

A FINAL WORD

The little girl in the train kept whispering to her mother. At last, the mother said exasperatedly, 'For the last time, please stop whispering and speak up.'

'Hasn't that man got a big red nose?' bellowed the child in a tone that could have been heard two compartments away.

*T*hat is what children are—innocent, sweet creatures. They can do you proud if you train them properly. But they can turn out to be the biggest embarrassments of your life, if you fail to do so.

"From the day your baby is born," counselled a famous scholar, "You must teach him good manners and correct values in life. In the absence of these, children today are becoming brats. They have no etiquette, flaunt authority and show scant respect to their elders. They no longer rise when their parents or superiors enter the room. Imagine the kind of awful creatures they will be when they grow up."

The scholar was none other than Socrates, who wrote these words in 399 B.C. And believe me, things haven't changed much since then. In this book, I have emphasized the need for teaching children good etiquette. We have dealt in this book exhaustively, with various situations, and the importance of reacting to them in a positive and socially acceptable manner.

Familiarity with the various norms and nuances of etiquette can make a person feel confident. But knowing how to do things right is not enough. You should also know how to do things efficiently. It requires practice. Everyday occasions provide ample opportunity to practice and perfect our manners.

So give your children enough space to move about, mix around and watch them grow into fine, cultured human beings. Remember, perfection may not come about overnight, but is certainly within reach.

A guide to good manners remains essentially what it is — a guide. So many cases and instances have to be judged on their own merit and you are the best person in the circumstances to determine the wisest approach to any situation.

SORRY!
THIS IS NOT ETIQUETTE!

Howsoever, well-mannered we might be, at one time or the other most of us fail the test of etiquette. Without even realising our mistake, we land up offending or irritating others by our lack of some basics of social behaviour. Here we are presenting a few situations of which lot of us are guilty at one time or the other. Can you spot yourself in these?

○ There was a newly appointed employee who tried to humour his boss by telling a joke. But much to his surprise instead of bringing a smile on his boss' face it only brought a frown. And it was only later, when pointed out by a friend, he realised that it was not his joke but bad breath that had caused this.

○ There was an avid telephone buff who would make long calls from his neighbourhood — and that too at odd hours. Only when he himself got a phone and neighbours came calling that he realised his folly.

○ A merry-go-round driver would zip past others' on the road without bothering about their convenience. One day when he was taking a walk on the roadside in his spotless white dress he got

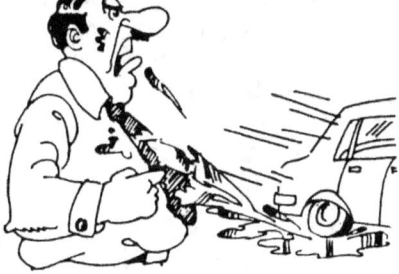

splashed with mud by a passing vehicle. And then he knew where he was wrong.

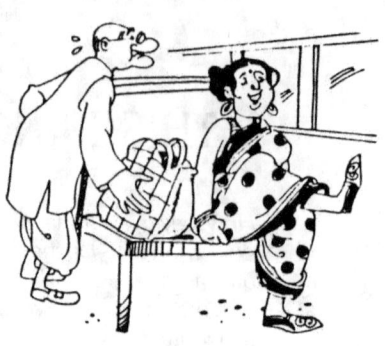

○ **U**nmindful of others' convenience, one lady would often get on to a bus and deposit whatever she had in hand on the seat next to her. Once when she put a big bag stuffed with all sorts of things on the seat and got pulled up by a co-commuter, that she realised her mistake.

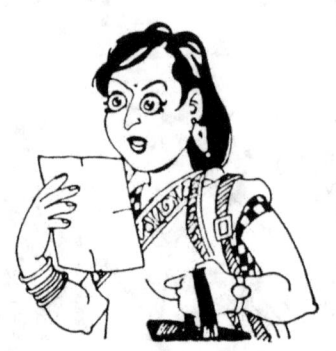

○ **O**ne young girl had a strange habit of prying into other people's affairs. Without realising that she was doing anything wrong, she would often open her friends purses, pry into their wardrobes and read their letters. One day she picked up a friend's letter she found that it contained lot of uncomplimentary reference to herself. And that cured her of this breach of manners.

○ **O**ne gentleman who was never taught any manners would deposit all his garbage in front of his neighbour's house. And then something happened that cured him of this practice for life. One day when he went past his neighbour's house he

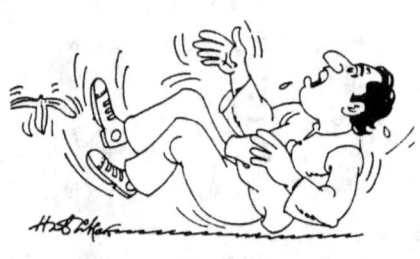

slipped badly on a banana peel and broke his leg. Ironically it was he who himself had dropped all that garbage that brought him down.

○ **O**ne young man was in the bad habit of visiting his relatives without properly preparing his baggage. He would inevitably land up borrowing toothpaste, soap, shaving cream, etc. from the host. Once he got a host who was one-up on him. He in turn started asking him for loans. And this corrected him of his bad habit.

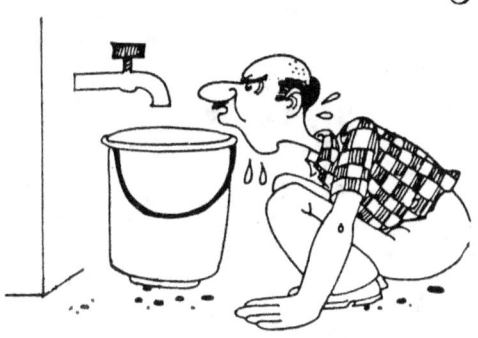

O **D**espite the fact that one gentleman had an adequate supply of water in his house, he installed a water pump simply to improve the pressure. Neighbours' complaints simply fell on deaf ears. Later he shifted his residence into another colony and he got a house on the second floor. Here everybody around — even the people at the ground floor — had motors, and he was left high and dry.

Of course there are many situations when you should take care to avoid embarrassment. Here are a few tips which will help to make you well-mannered:

O **D**on't make noise while eating food

O **D**on't talk in a library

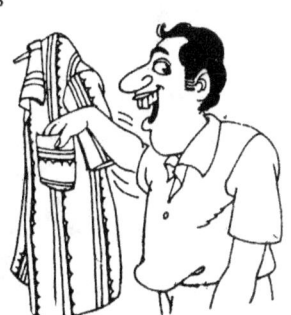

O **N**ever tear sheets from library books

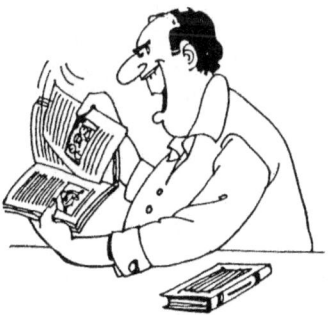

O **N**ever put hands in other people's pockets

○ **D**octors should not pass on their sample medicines to the patients

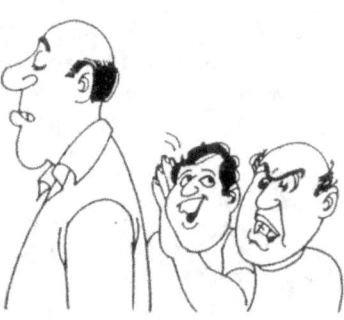

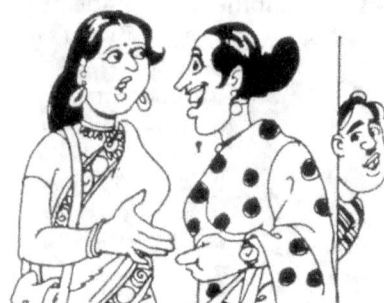

○ **D**on't eavesdrop on others

○ **D**on't indulge in backbiting

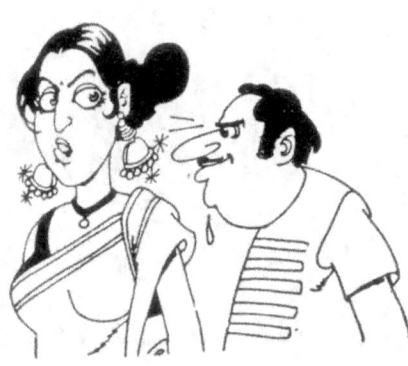

○ **N**ever stare at ladies

○ **S**low down your vehicle on the zebra crossing

○ **A**t a shop always wait for your turn. Don't break queue

○ **W**hile having meals with other people don't get up in between. Wait till everyone has finished with his meal

○ **D**on't disturb neighbours putting your music system on high volume

www.ingramcontent.com/pod-product-compliance
Lightning Source LLC
Chambersburg PA
CBHW052318220526
45472CB00001B/178

9 789381 384152